CONTENTS

CONVER-SATION with SCOTT RUFF

NINA RAPPAPORT: What inspired you to study architecture? How did you experience your first forays into the field?

SCOTT RUFF: I was part of a performance group outside of high school, and when we traveled I always drew. I also had an interest in math and science, and my guidance counselors put those together and said, "Oh, architecture!" My family didn't think it would be economical to go to school only for art, so architecture seemed like a good compromise. I'm from Buffalo, New York, and I wanted to go away for school, but not too far, so I applied to the Upstate schools and was accepted at Cornell University on the condition that I attend their precollege summer architecture program. That summer blew my mind in a good way because I found that I really enjoyed the craft—especially the way architects are asked to think outside the box. I was used to having definitive answers, and architecture was asking me to develop possible solutions. In my freshman design studio the professors taught through a Deconstructivist lens; I was not prepared for that.

NR What was a memorable project from that time?

SR The final project of the first semester was the "sound project," where they set up an entire sound studio in a room, with no explanation. They turned on a tape recorder and played three-and-a-half minutes of static and buzz sounds, asking us to place three-and-a-half interventions into these sounds. That was the moment that flipped my brain—being asked to analyze and translate information.

NR Much later, when you started to do more in-depth scholarship on the topics of identity and African-American culture, you wrote an essay about "signifying" inspired by Henry Louis Gates's analysis of culture and literature. Could you describe how you applied his idea of signification to architecture?

SR My approach to signifying comes from my reading of Darrel Fields's Architecture in Black and Gates's The Signifying Monkey, a seminal book on literary criticism. I found a great deal of relationship between how he positioned African-American literature both historically and today. I questioned whether there might be some connection between how African-American artists and designers borrow from their traditions, even if they weren't educated formally. And I questioned where one gets a formal education and when it actually begins. Why not begin talking about aesthetics in the home? It may not be framed within a particular tradition, but you form your own ideas from it. Reading books by authors such as Zora Neale Hurston was just part of my own development, along with ideas about spirituality that Gates tapped into. Signifying is a philosophy that really comes from a cosmology, an understanding of who we are in the universe.

NR In what way did you apply this theoretical literary strategy to architectural and spatial signifying—through engaging with program and site, rhetorical formal strategies, and references to history and culture? Is there a difference in spatial signification between African-American design culture and others, or do you find the same influences embedded everywhere?

SR I find them embedded everywhere; it is the way informed creative acts happen. In some ways it is a human condition: it's the hierarchy or emphasis different cultures place on different aspects of information. For example, humans can eat only within a certain set of foods. Poison to one set of humans is poison to another set of humans. This becomes an identification of the base materials that a culture is drawn from. What spices do they have access to? What have their experiences with other cultures been? All of that informs how dishes are prepared, resulting in different flavors in different cultures. In architecture it's very much the same. Regionalism is very important. Until very recently we haven't had a global culture accessing materials everywhere. You're informed by the availability of local materials and how you decide to draw upon a particular history. This is a very important component for how I look at history and talk about signifying. One architectural example is Thomas Jefferson's home, in Monticello, and the understanding of server versus served in the fundamental American tradition of hiding African Americans in relation to how white Americans design spaces for African Americans. Then we have ghettos as an urban condition at the other end of the scale. Just by looking at those two polarities we can start to discuss and construct a critique of African-American space within white space.

NR How do you relate cultural anthropology traditions, such as spiritual and regional references, to your architectural work? And how did your projects help you engage with and express culture in new ways that also connected to local cultures?

Scott Ruff, All Souls' Episcopal Church, long section, 2010

SR I started to tackle spirituality in architecture very early on. I was raised a Catholic and found the church to be the most beautiful space, leading to an interest in spiritual spaces of African religions. I found that they were not as formalized as in the Western tradition and could be developed almost anywhere. This, in turn, started to inform the way I think about architecture as not just a shelter but also a set of relationships through which spiritual and other forces come together. This approach played out in my New Orleans project for an informal Episcopal church that was a Walgreen's before Hurricane Katrina hit it in the Lower Ninth Ward. When I first moved there the congregation asked me to design a mural behind their altar, but they didn't have an altar, so we talked about a complete redesign of the entire sanctuary in terms of both the formal Episcopal church and the tradition of informal storefront churches. That project brought many things together for me since I drew upon regional materials from homes that were destroyed in the wake of Katrina.

NR How does the connection to a culture's spirituality play out in your design for the Guardians Institute at the Donald Harrison Sr. Museum?

SR This project was for the Mardi Gras Indians, a spiritual organization that comes together on a regular basis to worship through music, language, and African-American mystical traditions. The design references regional types such as the shotgun house, translating this information through spatial dialogue with the site, the interior program, and the need to project and perform. Unlike a contextual piece, it needs to stand out for the Mardi Gras Indians, and it has become an identifier for them.

NR What took you to New Orleans, and when did you move there?

SR I went in what was the "second line" of intervention after Katrina. There were the first responders, who went down in 2005–6 to build, but that started to dissipate very quickly when it was no longer fashionable. By 2009 I saw the need for more intervention and assistance, so I leaped at the opportunity to move down and teach at Tulane as well as engage with the community and culture. New Orleans has historically been a significant center of African-American cultural development, and the city was essential to my research on African-American aesthetics and architecture. I had the opportunity to engage the musical traditions and the vernacular of the shotgun house in what I've come to call a primordial African-American urban enclave (AAUE). I give it that acronym because so many people were offended by me using "ghetto" as a term.

NR What inspired you to teach, and how has it become the primary part of your practice as an architect?

SR Teaching is something I think I was meant to do. Architecture design studios are horribly taught on average, and architecture professors are not taught how to teach. At Cornell I engaged a great educator, Jerry Wells, who said, "No one ever taught you anything. They give projects out, and you are supposed to fly by the seat of your pants on talent." He proceeded to give me extra reading assignments steeped in the tradition of Colin Rowe. This set my mind afire. And as he taught me, I taught my African-American and Latino colleagues. We critiqued each other's work and became stronger as a set of students

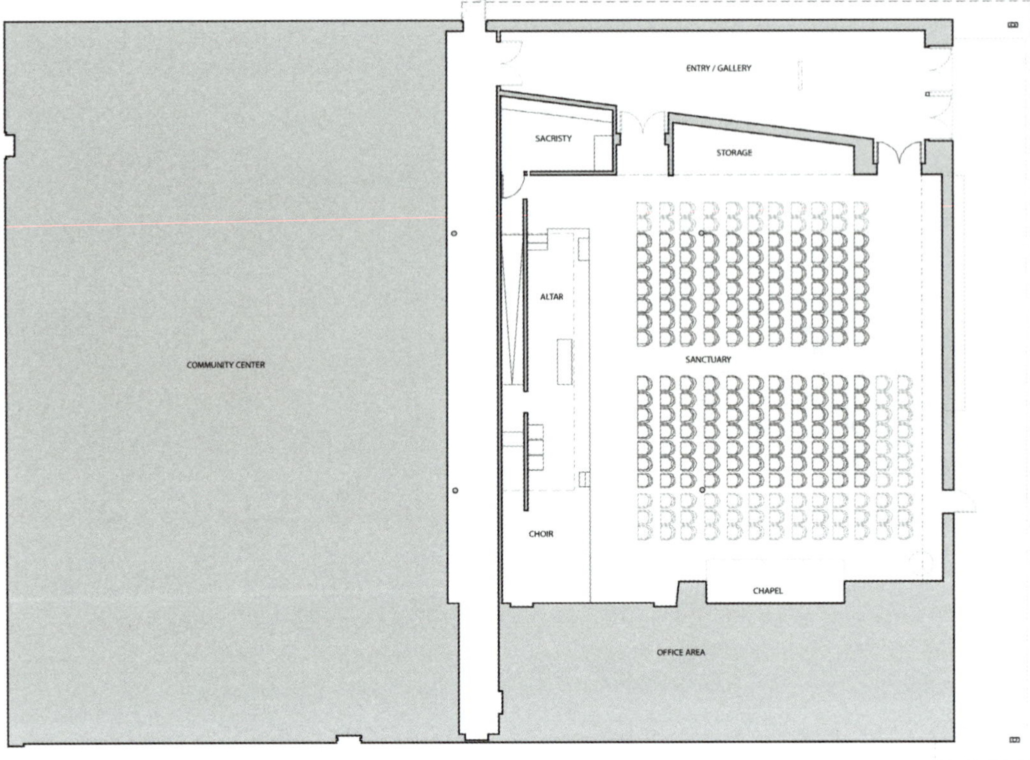

Scott Ruff, All Souls' Episcopal Church, plan, 2010

Scott Ruff, Guardians Institute, front elevation, 2012

through our Organization of Minority Architects, which attained recognition. I married teaching with my interest in African-American aesthetics, and that became my curriculum during my graduate fellowship at Cornell.

NR How do you teach issues of cultural identity to students who might not have formed their own identities yet and may not have backgrounds in cultural history?

SR I teach students how to leverage their own identities through their work. I employ my ways of accessing culture and identity, particularly African-American culture, and my processes as examples of the way they might look at their own cultures, and then I help them translate culture into spatial acts. That is my interest in teaching. I'm not interested in students taking on the African-American mantle per se. I'm interested in them contributing to the multicultural diversity of the human project by using aesthetics that we might all partake in.

NR Do you feel that the profession is diversifying and that educational institutions are reflecting that in their programs? How do we change the architecture population if we don't recruit a more diverse group of candidates?

SR I struggle with this every day. I work at elite institutions because I believe we need to crack the glass ceiling limiting the low number of tenured African-American architecture professors. Only about two percent of practitioners in the profession are African American, and for teaching it is even worse. The number of adjuncts makes it look like these people are around, but how can they effect change? It isn't easy to convince people to come to architecture and stay when they aren't represented.

NR What site and subject are you investigating now at Yale?

SR Since I so rarely engage in African-American projects, I'm looking at the possibility of two sites, one in the North and one in the South, where we can engage the narrative of the Underground Railroad and the idea of working with the mundane and the monumental as a binary relationship. How does one take the simple things in life and ritualize them—if they have not already been ritualized—and then translate that into space? The Underground Railroad was a clandestine activity, and thus not a lot of material culture has come out of it. What it has left is narrative. I'm really interested in translating narrative and a sense of legacy into spatial acts. I'm interested in rendering this significant historical event while talking about the differences between monumental, memorial, commercial, and spiritual spaces. We are going to look at spaces that have been reappropriated for use in a place in the South that was a starting point for the Underground Railroad and one in the North that was the ending point.

This discussion was published in the Fall 2017 issue of Constructs.

TOP: Scott Ruff, Guardians Institute, interior, 2012
BOTTOM: Scott Ruff, Guardians Institute, exterior, 2012

AFRO-(SURREALISM) SITUATIONIST

"Behold the invisible! You shall see unknown wonders!"

D. Scot Miller's Afrosurrealist Manifesto (2009) refers to Ralph Ellison's most famous novel, Invisible Man. This is not by accident. Ellison's "invisibility" is a social and phenomenological quality projected onto and experienced by peoples of African descent. The term Afro-Surreal was coined by writer and activist Amiri Baraka in the introduction to Henry Dumas's book Ark of Bones and Other Stories, published in 1974. He used it to describe Dumas's "skill at creating an entirely different world organically connected to this one ... the Black aesthetic in its actual contemporary and lived life." According to Baraka, "Afro-Surreal presupposes that beyond this visible world there is an invisible world striving to manifest, and it is our job to uncover it."

Keeping the tenets of the Afrosurrealist Manifesto in mind, the students were introduced to the Gullah Geechee, an African-American community whose roots and contemporary culture are traced to Africa as well as to the very inception of the United States of America. The Gullah Geechee enclave is a prime example of Afro-Surrealism: a hybridization of cultures that resists the erasure of an original way of life. Jean-Paul Sartre characterized the art of Léopold Sédar Senghor and the African Surrealist (or Negritude) movement as revolutionary and surrealist because it is black. Afro-Surrealism considers all "others" who create from their actual lived experience as surrealist. To manifest or formalize "black" people and experiences into the American public sphere is surreal.

The studio also engaged ideas of what is called Afro-Situationalism. Responding to constructed environmental conditions both immediate and systemic, Afro-Situationist modes of operation are primarily tactical, and its strategies are analytical and deconstructing, moving toward a hybridized reconstruction of current ways of life.

The studio was organized at a time of intense cultural stress related to identity politics in the United States. The presumed "postracial" new world order seemingly collapsed with the end of Barack Obama's two terms as president and the election of a culturally conservative regime. The evolution of social media and the ability to record and disseminate live video has armed African Americans with tools to expose entrenched abuses by law enforcement, government, employers, and citizens toward people of African descent. These platforms gave rise to the movement "Black Lives Matter." A common theme in many of these unfortunate video revelations is the propriety of the black body in public space. The dictating of whether and how a person of African descent should dwell in a specific location at a certain time is often a fundamental reason for being stopped, detained, assaulted, incarcerated, or even killed. The issue of blackness and space is brought to the national stage as the country deals with aggressive gentrification in historically African-American communities, further dislocating and politically disenfranchising the culture. Even the right to assemble and to protest is contested. This is evidenced in President Donald Trump's aggressive media assaults on peaceful protests of African Americans at "public" events, such as football games, where players have been penalized for kneeling during the national anthem.

Typical rice plantation in South Carolina, mid-1700s. Image from "The Economy of South Carolina" in The Crucial Decade: 1780s. M. S. Clark, December 6, 2012

> "I am an invisible man. ... I am invisible, understand, simply because people refuse to see me. ... When they approach me they see only my surroundings, themselves, or figments of their imagination—indeed, everything and anything except me."
> —Ralph Ellison, Invisible Man, 1965

One of the primary tools used by the African-American community to counter the abhorrent treatment of its people and render itself visible is spatial and situationist. Public assembly and protest in both designated and undesignated locations create disruptions of space in the streets of cities, blocking highways and town squares. Even silence and refusal to participate in cultural ceremonies disrupts the flow of sanctioned behavior in space. The African-American community's request for the removal of monuments celebrating the legacy of racial and cultural oppression from public spaces created the context for a studio focused on social justice. The effects of this national atmosphere were manifested on the Yale University campus when recent protests precipitated the rechristening of Calhoun College, named after a notorious proponent of slavery, and coincidentally a South Carolinian.

Charleston, South Carolina, is one of the country's great tourist cities. From the late seventeenth to the nineteenth century it was arguably the most important economic port in the nation. To tour the city is to learn the story of its formation and development. Buildings that have stood the test of time, institutions, sculptural monuments, and museums stand as physical signs of the proud colonial and postcolonial role the city played in the early formation of the nation. Rice, indigo, cotton, and slave markets enabled the city to develop into an economically powerful and cultured city.

This context prompts the question: "Where is the space for people of African descent?" Like many places in the United States, Charleston can be read as at least two separate cultural spaces. One is highly visible and curated for a romantic image of a genteel "white" culture with colonial origins, while the other operates in tandem with the carefully cultivated environment but is virtually invisible.

Architecture is a social and political enterprise, despite a general insistence on the abstract and universal nature of the built environment. It will always be driven by who is designing and for whom, why the space is being designed, and how it is made. In academic settings projects are developed to address a predetermined programmatic issue or problem coupled with a methodological approach. In that regard, this architecture studio is not different. Where it differs is in the existence of two disparate aspects operating in a provisional state prepared for mutation as situational knowledge increases. Situational knowledge pertains to cultural, political, social, and environmental arenas of knowledge. When I first introduced the studio, I assumed the students had a sense of African-American culture, with all the baggage that might come with it. I was mistaken. African-American culture was an abstraction, an unknown other filtered and distorted through a Western colonial lens. This made the discussion about the Gullah Geechee community even more perplexing.

TOP: Carolina Gold rice grains

MIDDLE: Sweetgrass basket made by the Gullah culture of coastal Georgia and South Carolina

BOTTOM: Sweetgrass basketmaking

Many students initially understood the studio as a social-justice problem-solving exercise. Due to the cultural, political, and geographic context of the project, social justice was a de facto aspect of what the studio produced in terms of architectural research and propositions. An extant Maroon culture's continued struggle against erasure and for legitimacy and sovereignty in twenty-first-century South Carolina rings of political activism. But at the core of the project is property. The Gullah Geechee culture's history and practices are inextricably connected to place, necessitating ownership and development of the land. Beyond the apparent and immediate realities of Gullah Geechee life, the studio launched an ontological inquiry into the essence of the wider African-American and American contexts. The Gullah Geechee emerged from extreme acts of pragmatism as a reaction to the realities of individual and collective survival in a hostile environment. The community brings together survival, continuance, and remembrance of fragmented cultures, sometimes unnaturally. The Gullah Geechee are one of many "not so" missing links to the people of African descent in the United States.

The agenda of the studio was to develop architectural languages in which the social, political, and historical narratives operate as a conceptual foil and source for formal studies of Gullah Geechee culture. The studio operated at a complex three-part intersection within architectural discourse: formalism, phenomenology, and social activism. Each project developed a type of creole or pidgin architecture to reconcile the disparate positions. These architectural expressions were consciously developed from source material specific to the Gullah Geechee culture intermixed with contemporary African-American sociopolitical issues.

STUDIO BRIEF

Located off the coast of South Carolina and Georgia is a series of landmasses known as the Sea Islands. Among them islands such as Hilton Head are considered some of our country's most desirable beach retreats. These islands are also the ancestral home of the Gullah Geechee, an African-American people for whom the coastal region became a refuge where a communal culture developed. The Gullah Geechee community is deeply tied to West African traditions, and its religion, food, and language are amalgams of influences. This is partly due to a longstanding lack of vehicular access to the islands, allowing what the community's political representative, Queen Quet, has referred to as insulation, as opposed to mere isolation.

For more than seventy years this once relatively safe space of the Gullah Geechee culture has been under siege from developers and the cultural oppression of racism and classism. The community faces a number of pressures that threaten its traditions, self-sufficiency, geographic integrity, economic well-being, and community cohesion. These include the construction of bridges, increased secularization, the information age, and population dispersion to other parts of the country. However, the largest threat facing the Gullah Geechee is development. The unique and vital culture is disappearing and is in imminent danger of being erased entirely.

The plight of the Gullah Geechee ancestral lands is familiar because it reflects a problem plaguing contemporary African-American communities across the nation: gentrification. Historically the Gullah Geechee people have inhabited land deeded to them following the Civil War. Following the 1957 construction of the Sea Pines resort and a gated residential community on Hilton Head, the Sea Islands have seen an enormous influx of outsiders. The islands have been almost completely transformed into affluent, and white, vacation and retirement communities. A major contributing factor in this shift has been the legal status of heirs' property. Following the post–Civil War transfer of land, very few members of the Gullah Geechee community had wills, and consequently property rights have been distributed across generations of descendants. If even one party wishes to accept a developer's offer, the entire property is often forced into sale due to partition laws, the lack of legal assistance, and the inability of other descendants to buy out other shares because of the extremely high market value of land. In addition to displacement, development and tourism have shifted the Gullah Geechee economy away from independent agriculture and fishing to low-income service work in the tourism sector. Moreover, demographics on the Charleston peninsula are changing and census records reflect the displacement of the Gullah Geechee community: data from 2000 shows the area was 52 percent African American and 45 percent non-Hispanic white; today those numbers stand at 72 percent Caucasian and 25 percent African American.

The studio addressed issues of sustainability, both cultural and environmental, and explored the notion that the material and ideological production of a single culture is a source of architectural ideas. We explored how the Gullah Geechee culture was able to survive in semi-isolation for approximately 150 years. Language and sustenance are as important as the climate, landscape, and artifacts of a landscape to producing a cohesive sense of place.

Research

"Research is formalized curiosity. It is poking and prying with a purpose."
—Zora Neale Hurston

"Creativity requires input, and that's what research is. You're gathering material with which to build."
—Gene Luen Yang

Research is defined as the systematic investigation into and study of materials and sources to establish facts and reach new conclusions. The students were asked to conduct an extensive investigation into the coastal Gullah Geechee. The product of the research first manifested as presentations that the students shared with each other. Through observation and interpretation of gathered information, the students determined standards for how the data was to be interpreted into a concise presentation. This task required resourcefulness and curiosity since each group gathered information on topics ranging from geography, agricultural production, and vernacular architecture to traditional crafts, cuisine, belief systems, and ethnic origins of the communities.

TOP: Charleston's Forgotten Quays. A detail of a Charleston map from 1855 indicates the owners of the docks, which correspond to those of plantations around the Sea Islands. Many of these names remain in the city as those of streets that were once quays.

BOTTOM: John Stobart's painting of the Old Exchange as a place for trading goods and people

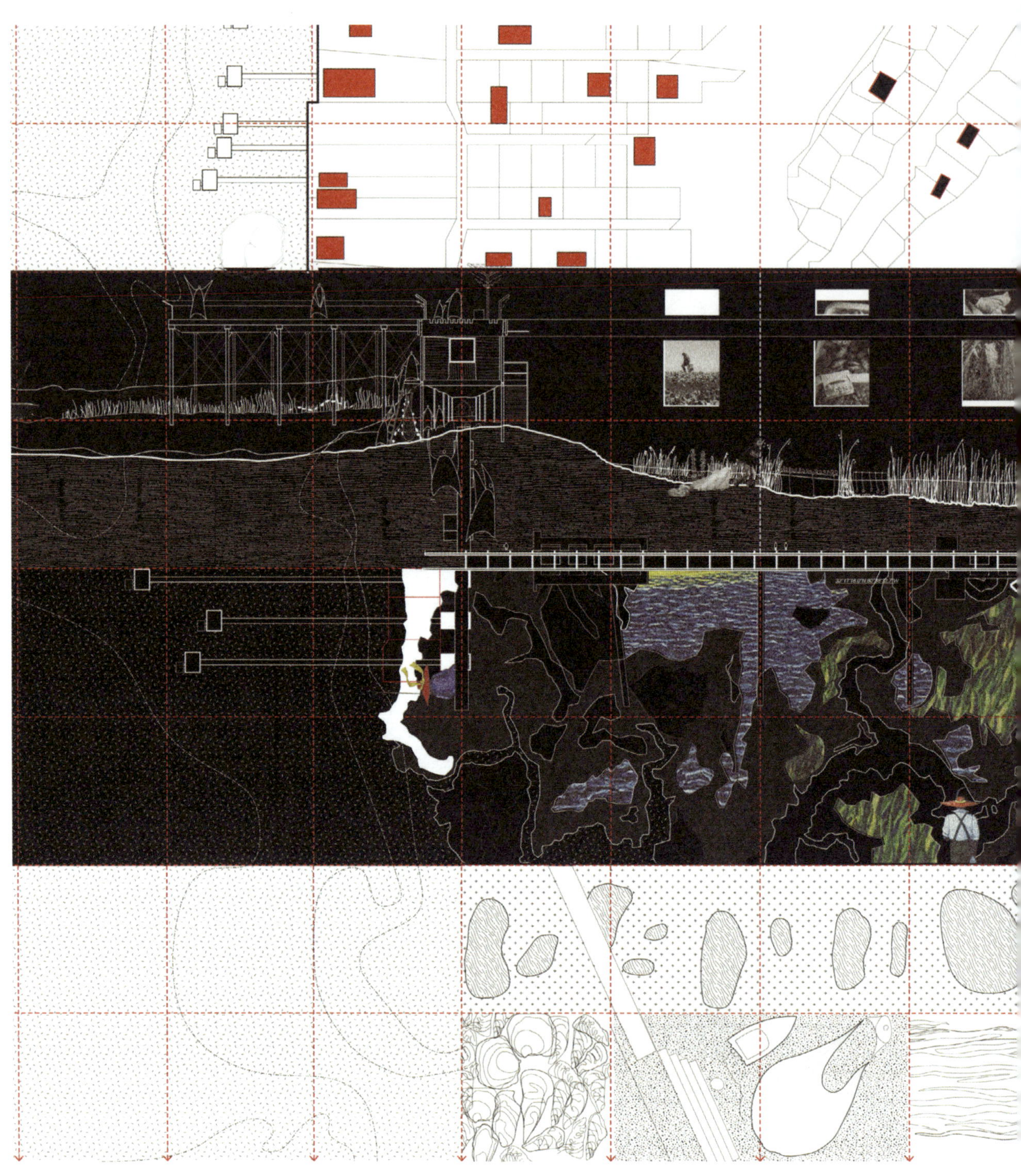

Site plan and section drawing exploring the changing ecological and social site composition of St. Helena Island

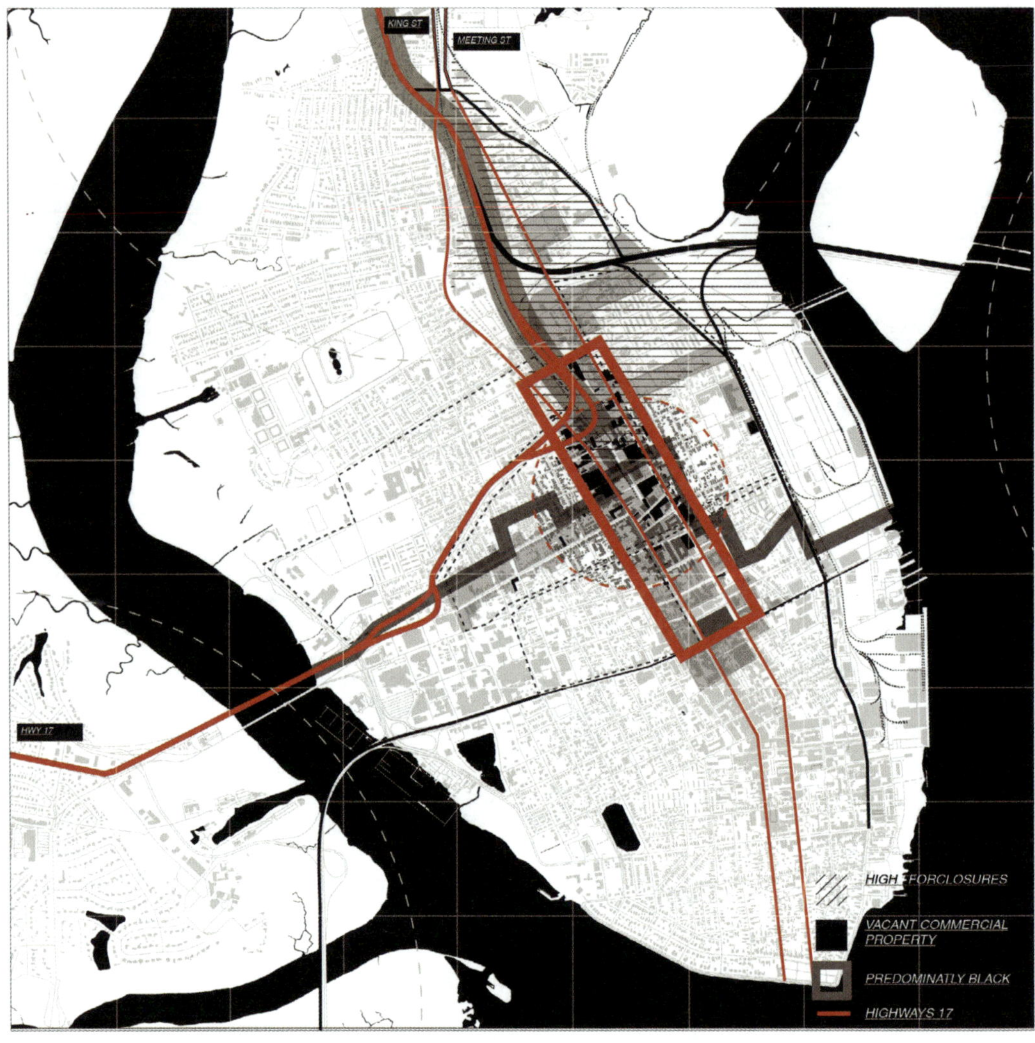

Diagram of the proposed low-line and urban wetland located at the racial and economic border between north and south Charleston. This border is defined by the physical boundaries of urban-renewal infrastructure Highway 26, which displaced African-American populations during its construction in the mid-twentieth century.

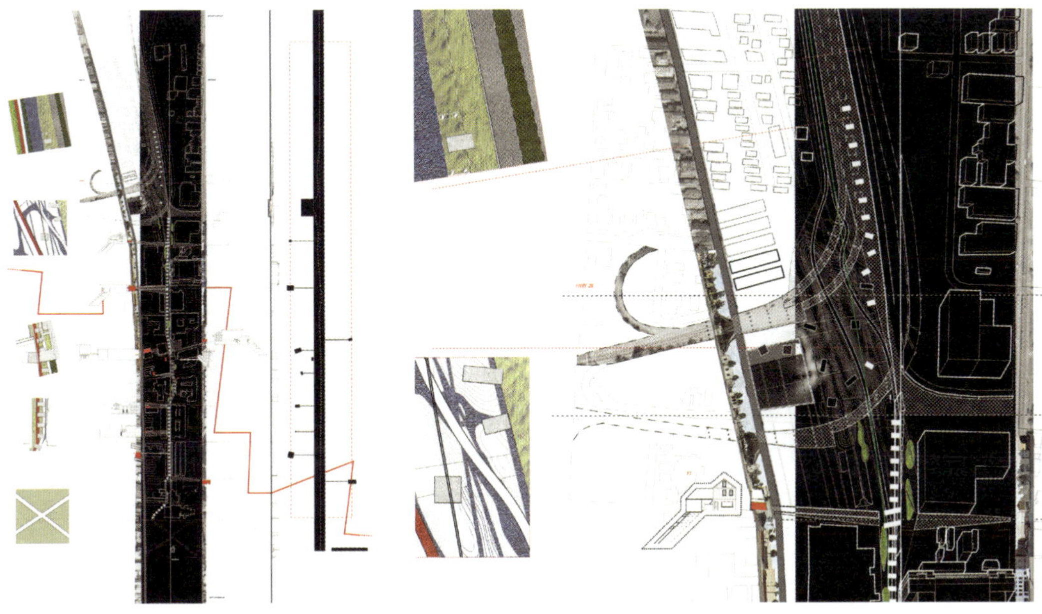

Site plan of Charleston's low-line bike and pedestrian path, urban wetland, and gateway interventions proposed for vacant lots as part of a community land trust

Travel

The studio traveled to five locations in the Gullah Geechee Cultural Heritage Corridor of South Carolina and Georgia, including Charleston County, Beaufort, St. Helena Island, Hilton Head, and Savannah. Each location was chosen to engage particular ways Gullah Geechee culture has been influenced by and has in turn transformed the urban landscape of Charleston. The Sea Islands offered a unique location for the study of architecture and its role as a cultural signifier. Canonical examples of Euro-American settlements in the region clearly established a formal and spatial identity for the United States, in places like Savannah and Charleston as well as resort towns such as Myrtle Beach and Hilton Head. African-American Gullah Geechee history is embedded in these locations. The purpose of the research was to reveal the remnants of that cultural space and graphically communicate the information through critical architectural drawings, diagrams, and models of material artifacts and places.

The trip transformed many students' ideas about the sites and cultural focus. We took guided tours of Charleston, St. Helena Island, and Savannah. The students investigated their proposed sites of interest in Charleston and St. Helena Island. In Charleston we visited the Avery Research Center, an African-American cultural research facility, and learned about the contemporary issues of gentrification in the region. Students were able to clarify the issues related to the problem of "heirs property," the policy under which land has been taken and gentrified in the Sea Island region. On St. Helena we met with Marquetta Goodwine, or Queen Quet, the elected "chieftess" of the Gullah Geechee nation. She honored us by leading our tour across the island and imparted her vast knowledge of many topics related to Gullah Geechee geopolitical issues.

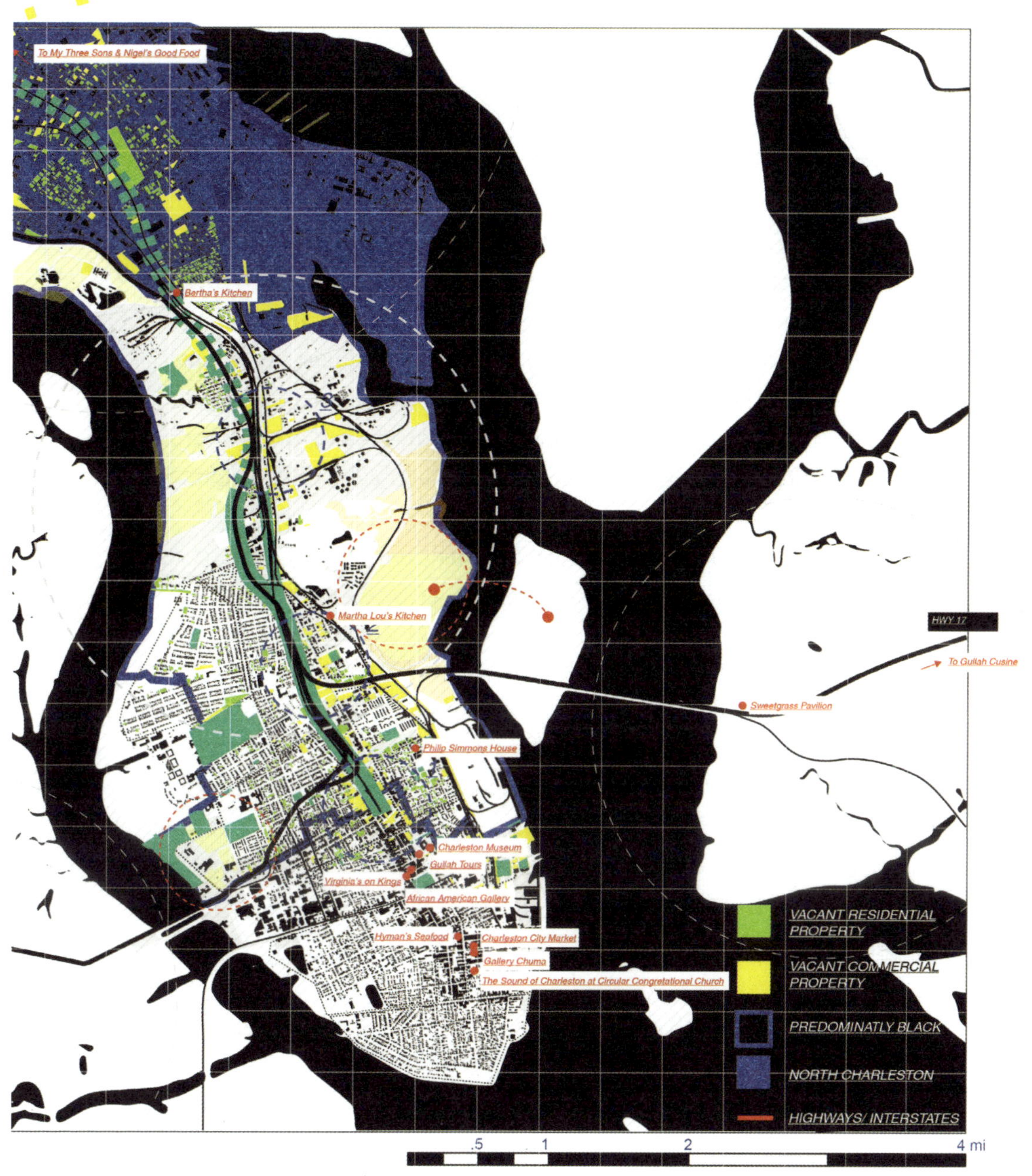

The Charleston site, highlighted with a blue dotted circle, is located at the nexus between the predominantly black northern neighborhoods and southern wealthier neighborhoods, which were historically occupied by black communities. As development and tourism expand at the southern tip so too does the gap between African-American neighborhoods and the city center.

Project

The studio engaged two primary architectural issues: a critique of historic and contemporary museum typology and the translation of cultural ideas into tectonic and spatial strategies. Students were tasked to create a formal introduction, or gateway, into the Gullah Geechee corridor for a fictional organization called the Gullah Geechee Society of Charleston. The building was to have a hybrid program operating between the typologies of museum, monument, memorial, and cultural center to preserve, promote, and perpetuate Gullah Geechee tradition and history into the future. It would be a way for the community to control the information and messages disseminated to the public as well as be a resource and archive for its members.

Each student developed a program for a Gullah Geechee institute that responded to the fundamental need for the group to articulate its history (the past), maintain its traditions (the present), and pass its legacy on to the next generation (the future). For the Gullah Geechee the facility would not be just a museum, a school, a company, or a theater—it would be all those things and more. The program would reflect the culture as a multiperspectival hybrid of varied components comprising an enigmatic and poetic whole.

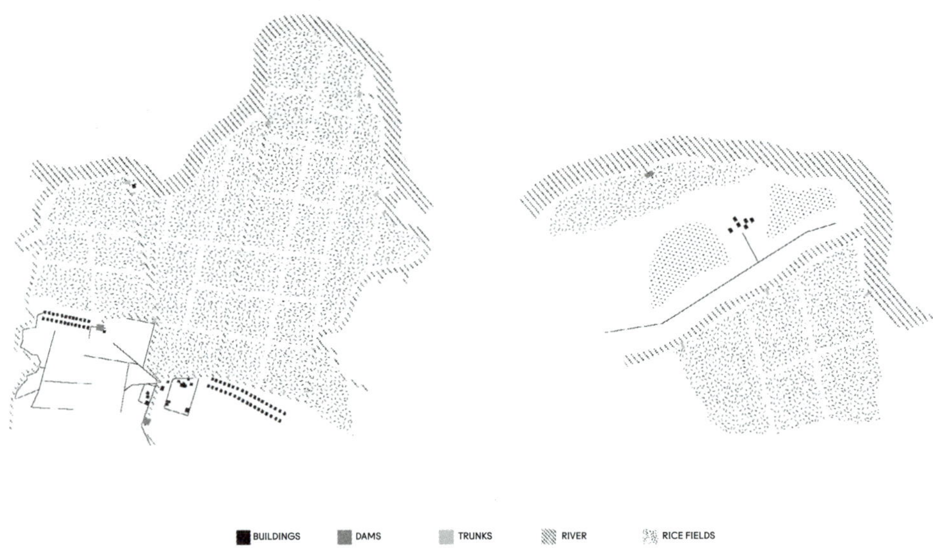

ABOVE: Map of permanent and temporary African-American gathering spaces on the Charleston peninsula

OPPOSITE: Left: A typical plantation, organized linearly in contrast to the composition of traditional Gullah Geechee compounds. Right: The unique physical form of the Gullah compound is strengthened by the close functioning of family groups. Centrally located in organic arrangements, buildings do not follow property boundaries.

Program Development

"Programs are as old as architecture. The first Greek temples began with program, not form. Most architects are blinded by form and ignore the potential of programs to generate forms. Think of department stores and railway stations in the 19th century: programs came first. It's the same with the merging of airports and shopping malls today."
—Bernard Tschumi

After a careful analysis of the context, each student proposed a programmatic model for the Gullah Geechee Institute. They were asked to imagine a formula of subprograms that combined the following macroprograms: community, education, commercial, residential, service, and outdoor areas. As a point of departure the students were to critically distill and extract the information captured during the first weeks of research and travel. Each design project explored varied strategies to define a particular relationship between culture, form, site, and program to challenge and inform what cultural architecture might be.

Gadsden's Wharf.

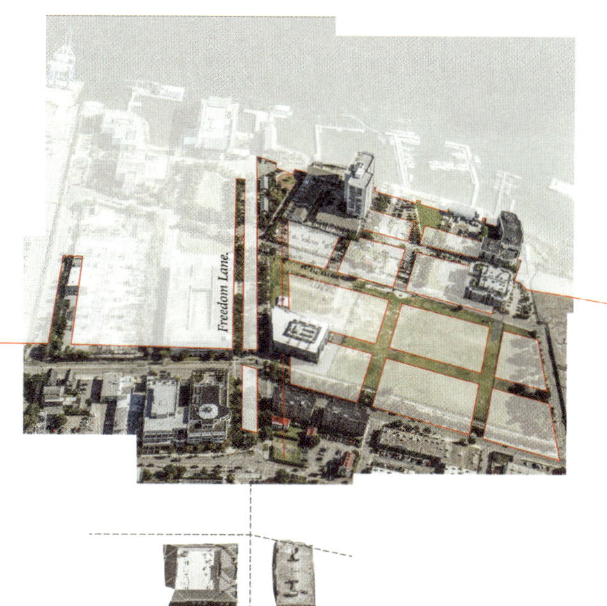

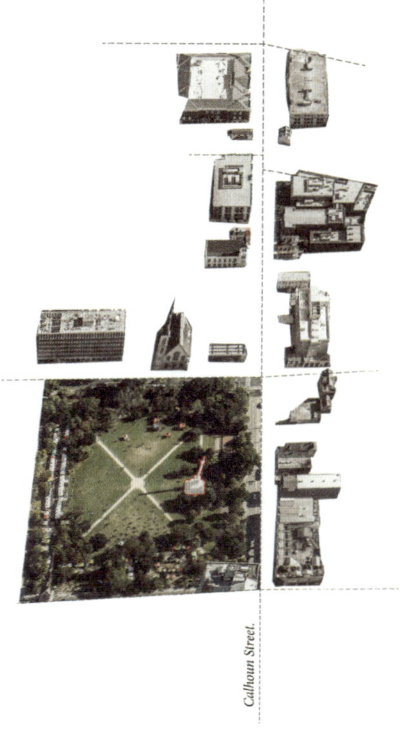

Merion Square.

ABOVE: Charleston celebrates a heroic history of wealth and power but barely whispers its horrific legacy of inhumane slave trading and enslavement. Few understand that it was the site of the largest influx of slaves to the Americas or that the region continues to dispossess its African-American population.

OPPOSITE: The Chapel of Ease's past shows that moments of African-American history connect to moments of the Gullah Geechee identity, including the Port Royal Experiment, a precursor to the educational programming proposed for the site.

STUDENT WORK

Meghan Royster Memorial Campus

Charleston's gentrification and shifting demographics create a critical need for a permanent urban gathering space for the Gullah Geechee people. Market stands "pop up" on the corners of existing stores or hotels and in the small side yards of buildings during the weekly Marion Square farmer's market. Since the number of out-of-towners exceeds that of local residents on the peninsula, there are large gaps in outlets for commercial and cultural exchange. Without the right infrastructure and community assistance, opportunities for cultural promotion are limited. Located in the quickly gentrifying neighborhood of Radcliffeborough, the site offers easy access to the local community and tourists through the nearby visitor's center.

The project's porous ground floor enables visitors to easily cross the site or access the different programmatic pavilions. From entrances on both King and St. Philip's Streets, visitors are directed through the spaces via a variety of circulation pathways. Each larger pavilion connects to a smaller one through a bridge, creating pedestrian paths above ground level. From the Charleston visitor's center people experience the campus from left to right, as represented in the unfolded section. Visitors first enter from King Street through the Visitor's Pavilion and then go through the marketplace to the Education Pavilion, through the gallery to the Performance Pavilion, and then exit onto King Street. Those entering from the Radcliffeborough neighborhood experience the campus from right to left, entering from St. Philip's Street through the community lounge to the Performance Pavilion, through the gallery to the Education Pavilion, and through the marketplace before exiting onto St. Philip's Street.

This project seeks to reclaim a space for people to gather while connecting the Gullah Geechee and other members of the local community with visitors who wish to understand a more inclusive history. With multiple centers in a variety of scales, an open ground-floor level, a sequencing of spaces emphasizing movement through the site, and a focus on landscape, this cultural campus is a living memorial that services, rather than simply signifies, a vibrant culture through opportunities of exchange and education.

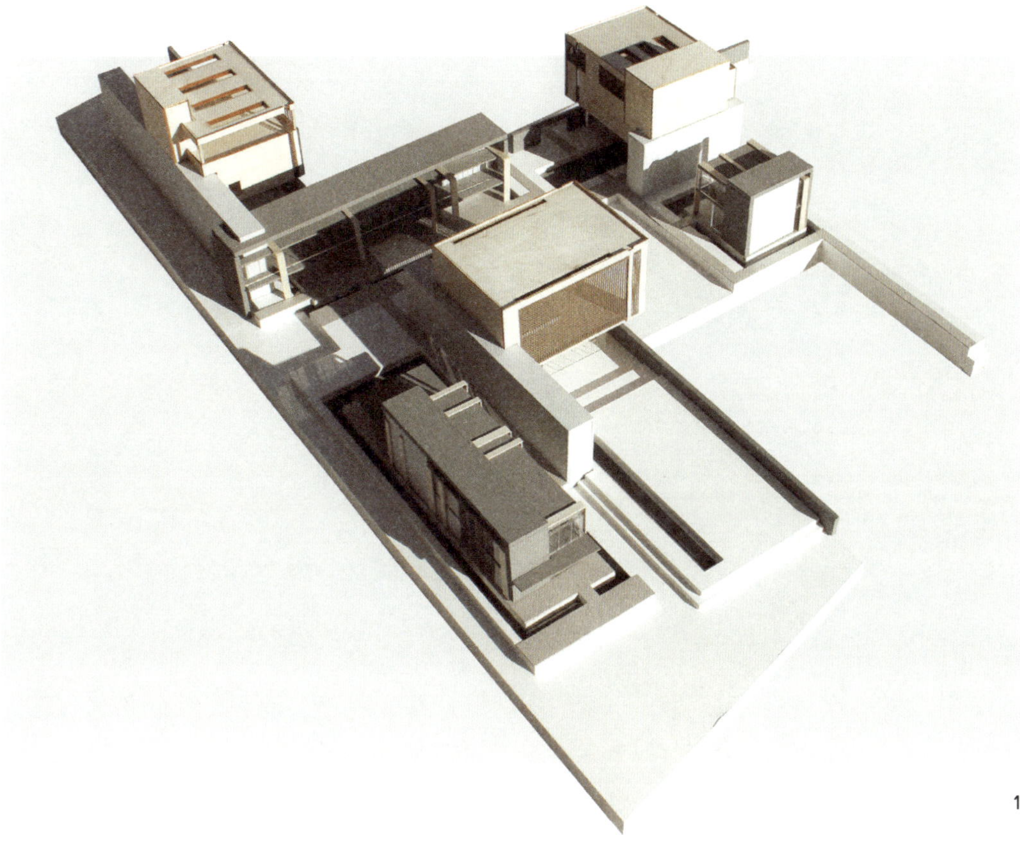

1

1 Model at 1/16″ scale with materials demonstrating the textures and intimacy of campus spaces. The St. Philip's Street entrance leads to the community lounge.

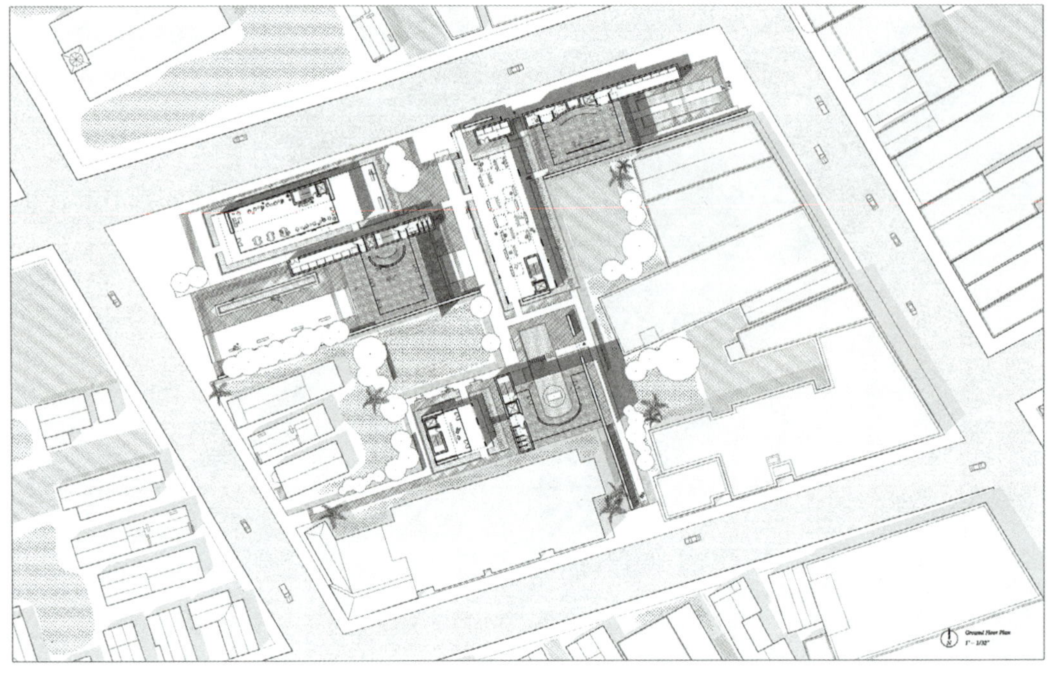

2

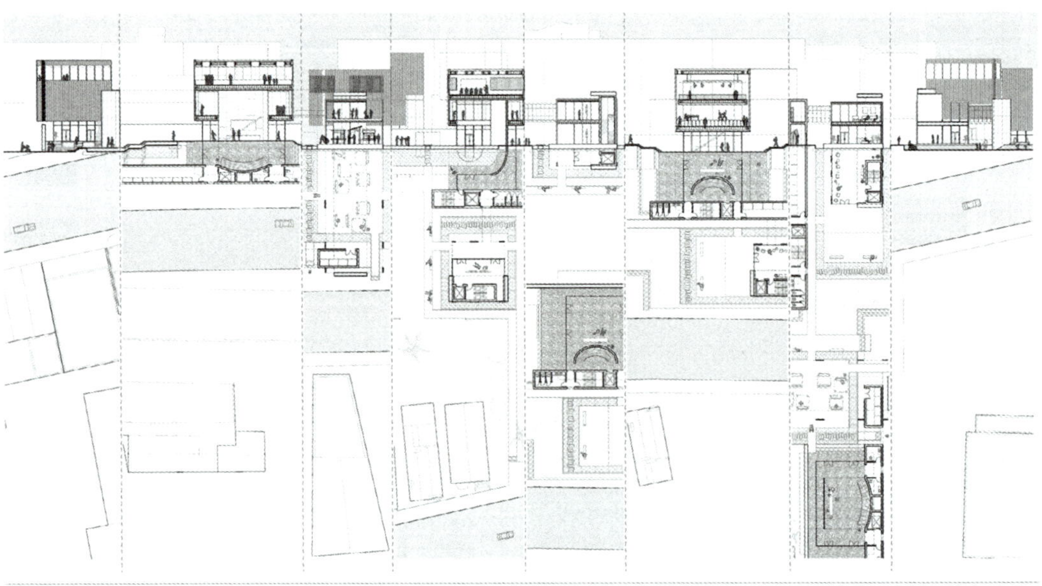

3

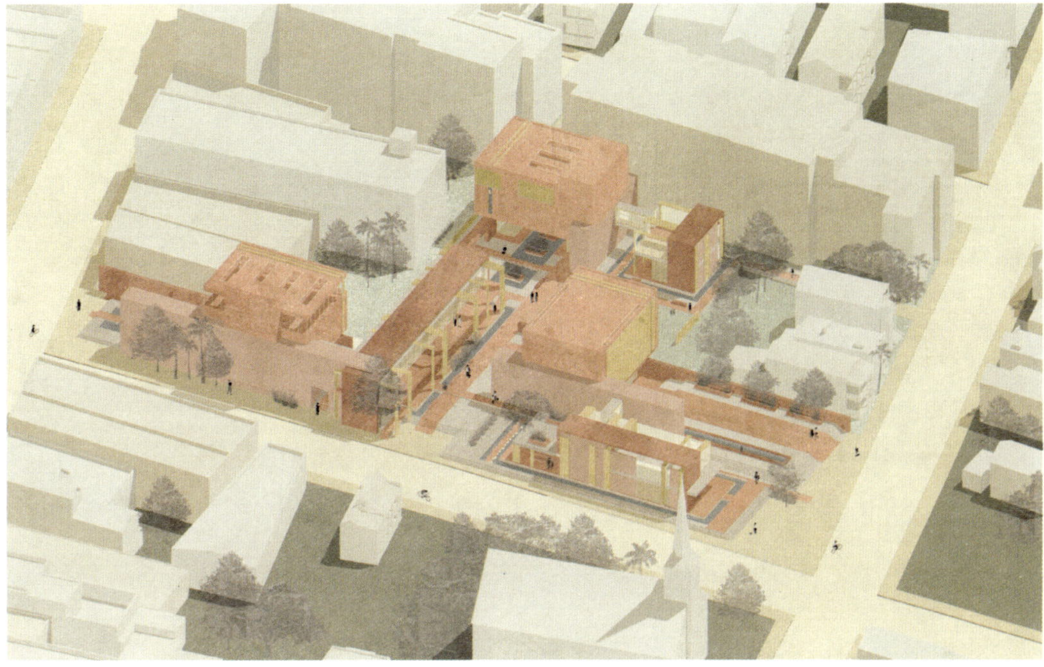

4

5

2 Ground-floor plan showing porous ground floor and spatial sequence

3 Section showing sequence of entry and circulation from each side of the site

4 Axonometric drawing of the Living Memorial Campus for the Gullah Geechee

5 The marketplace, where community members can rent space and display or sell crafts

6

7

8

6 St. Philip's Street, where the community enters from the surrounding neighborhood

7 Performance Pavilion from St. Philip's Street, where visitors and community members can watch or perform traditional Gullah Geechee dances

8 King Street front, where public enters the Visitor's Pavilion

Jonathan Molloy and Samuels Zeif
Charleston's Forgotten Wharf

Gadsden's Wharf is site of the oldest and most significant slave port in North America, where between forty and sixty percent of all kidnapped Africans arrived on the continent. It is at the terminus of Calhoun Street, the central artery of Charleston, and is home to the Fort Sumter Civil War museum and a banal green space, known as Liberty Park. There are only two small plaques commemorating the horrors of the slave trade that took place there.

"I believe unconditionally in the ability of people to respond when they are told the truth. We need to be taught to study rather than believe, to inquire rather than affirm," wrote Septima Clark, a Charleston hero who is memorialized by the crosstown highway that split apart this historically black neighborhood—an act of erasure as memorial.

We propose that preservation is not the presentation of a frozen history through vertical surfaces that defend what is already built, but the revealing of an ongoing history. It is a productive, not preventative, act. In contrast to facades, plaques, and monuments that mark but rarely change things, a living preservation engages the perpetuity of history in the present and into the future. As Christine Sharpe asks, "How does one mourn the interminable event?"[1] The typical mode of dealing with the past in the city is either a monument or a museum. Although significant as memorials, both practices suffer from the same inability to participate in the collective consciousness of the city beyond their physical presence.

What if we deal with the past instead through the appropriation of existing conditions? Appropriation derives significance from an active interface with its site, both culturally and physically. Weary of eliminating the human obligation to remember through material form, we advocate occupying space, not just marking it.

Our project aims to uncover the erasure of the slave port at Gasden's Wharf through a counter act of productive preservation. Gadsden's Wharf has the potential for two kinds of cultural occupation. First, we can uncover the material remains of the historic site, both as an academic investigation and as a symbolic process of uncovering an overwhelmingly ignored history. Second, we can bolster the ongoing work of the Avery Research Center for African American History and Culture, whose archive and scholarship is compromised by a lack of funding, space, and constant risk of flooding. Revealing the hallowed ground of the historic wharf and its canal would create a memorial precinct of archaeological excavation and archival research. The embedded museum would provide access to never before excavated sites of mass burials and building foundations, and an archival tower would sanctify the ongoing material research of African-American history and culture through visual juxtaposition: the city of arrival, the sea that delivered the arrivals from Africa, and the horizon that was left behind. It would be the tallest building in Charleston. At its base, a new ferry launch to Sullivan's Island marks both the point of the first arrival and St. Helena Island, a symbol of continuing survival.

1. Christine Sharpe On Blackness and Being (Durham, N.C.: Duke University Press, 2016)

1

2

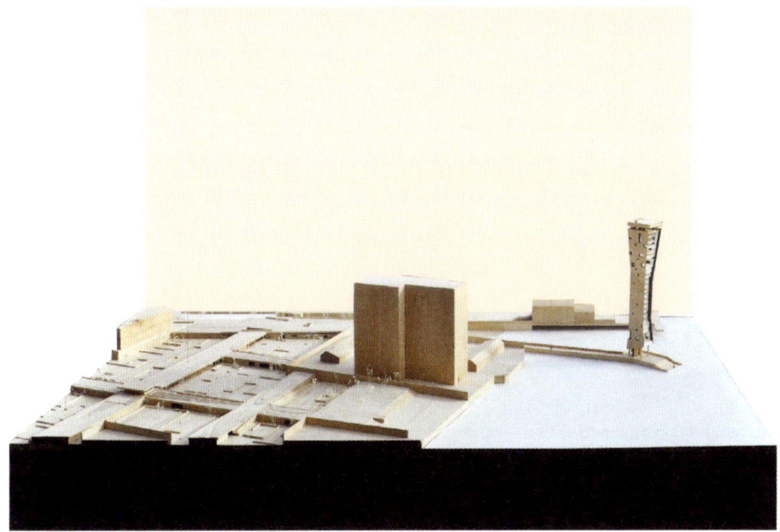

3

1 While the archaeological precinct explores the long forgotten histories of the ground, the tower celebrates the ongoing scholarship at places like the Avery Institute, whose important collections are constantly threatened by flooding and disrepair. The tower apotheosizes documents and artifacts in the sky to the level of the city whose history it represents.

2 America has never taken on the project of excavating its African-American history. Instead its locations have been purposefully erased and built upon, whether a slave burial site or an important building foundation. Through excavation and reconstruction, the new monument takes shape in a continuous act of discovery.

3 A memorial excavation precinct and an archival tower occupy the site.

4

4 The countermonument is concerned with the appropriation of an existing condition. It is by definition reactionary and cannot be the reason for its own being. Here it manifests from the reality of the ground and the truths it holds.

5 The archival tower, publicly accessed through the memorial canal, provides a relationship with the water and a view of the city. At its base a new ferry launch will send and receive boats to Sullivan's and St. Helena Islands. The first was the primary site of arrival, where slaves were held in "pest houses" until deemed healthy enough for arrival in Gadsden's Wharf. The second is the site for continuing survival of the Gullah Geechee culture, which has evolved on and around the Sea Islands.

6 With varying degrees of containment and porosity, the monolithic walls of the tower carefully hold and celebrate the documents and artifacts of its contextual history.

5

6

Pierre Thach
Gullah Geechee Kindergarten

This project proposes a new complex for living activities in East Charleston within the existing road infrastructure. For decades the Old Cooper River Bridge was popularly perceived as an urban scar in the heart of the Charleston peninsula. The crossing has since been removed and replaced by the Arthur Ravenel Jr. Bridge, located north of the site. A relatively large and underutilized series of lots now sits in its place, threatened by rising waters.

The Gullah Geechee Kindergarten responds to the need for a preschool educational facility to provide a place of cultural sustainability for the imperiled Gullah Geechee community of Charleston. A network of boardwalks wraps around the neighborhood and provides links to existing transportation routes. The kindergarten serves as the primary gateway from Meeting Street to this new green infrastructure. The circuit connects residents to key community programs of the neighborhood, beginning with Martin's Park, in the northern portion of the site, the St. Julian Devine Community Center to the east, and the bike lane of the Arthur Ravenel Jr. Bridge.

1

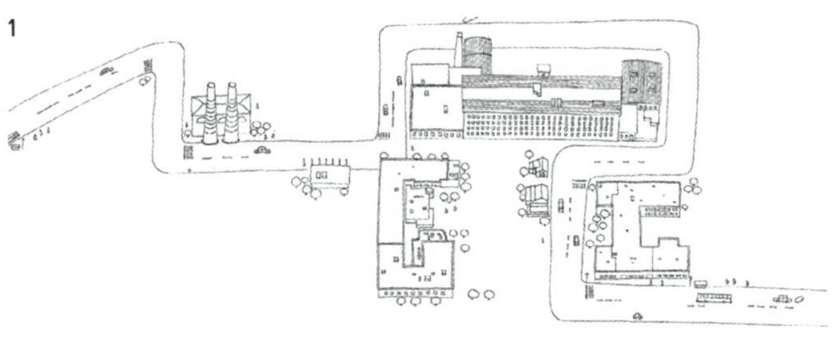

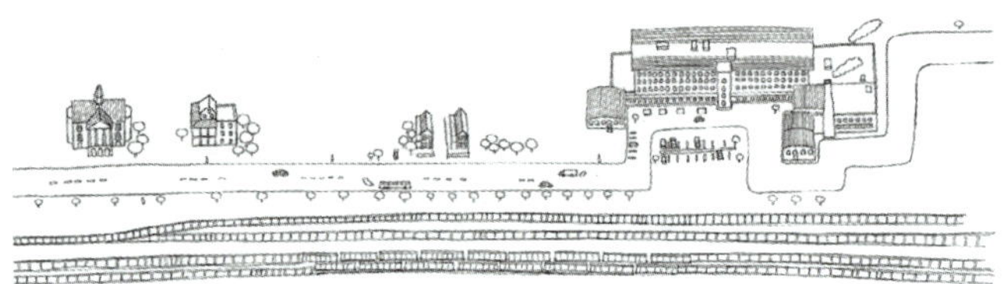

1 Site sketches of current activities

2 Oblique plan

3 Future flood risk

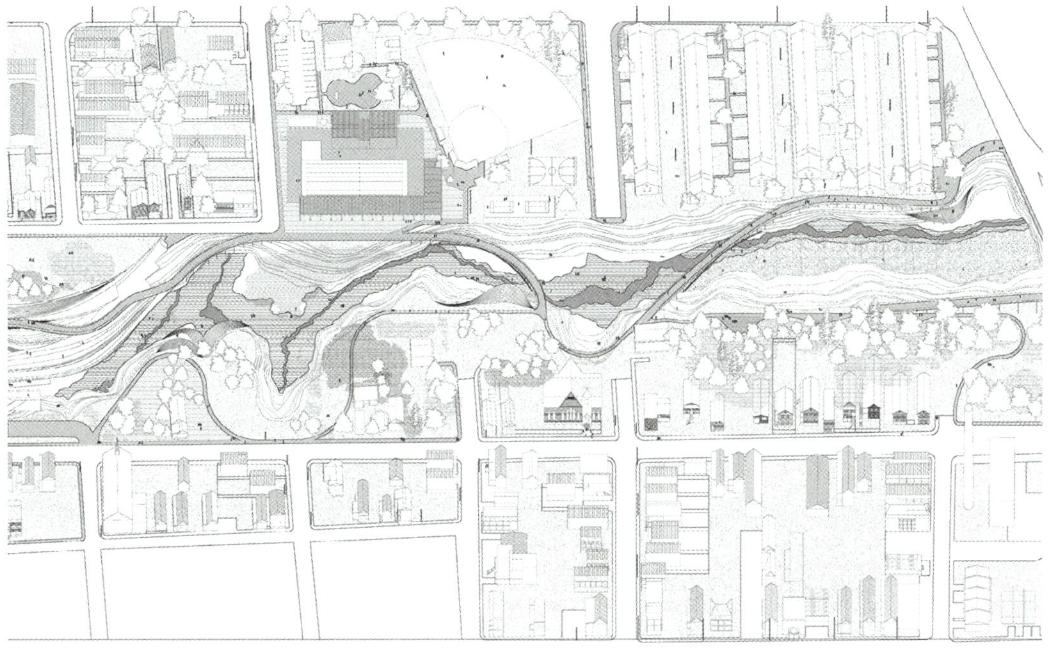

2

3

4

5

6

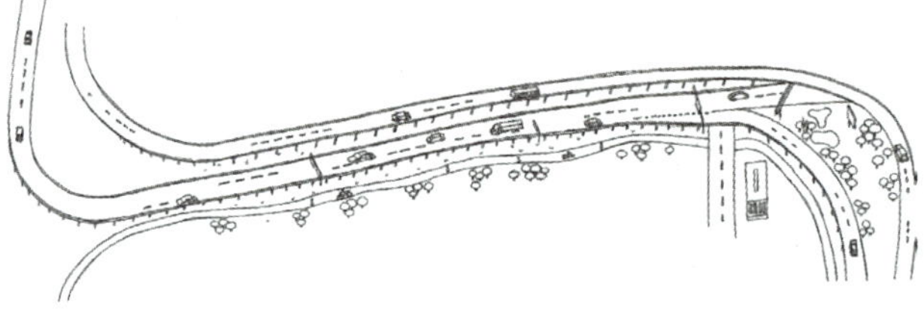

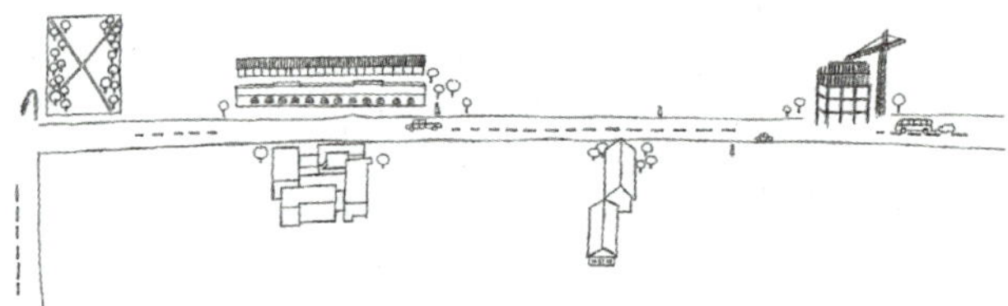

4 Model (previous spread)

5 Model

6 Current pedestrian and auto infrastructure supporting transportation and recreation

Abena Bonna
St. Helena's Chapel of Ease

The Gullah Geechee people of the Sea Islands have a traumatic history, and their cultural memory is fragmented into pieces. Where did they come from? What is their old identity? Where are they going? What will their new lives be like? St. Helena's Chapel of Ease has been a space of oppression, assimilation, societal mobility, and cultural agency. Built to serve the families of plantation owners who settled on St. Helena Island in the mid-1700s, the chapel was appropriated by formerly enslaved families when the owners evacuated the island during the Civil War. It was converted to a schoolhouse as part of the Reconstruction-era Port Royal Experiment to educate freedmen before a fire damaged it beyond repair in 1886. In this project the ruins of the chapel go through a series of deconstruction operations and are transformed into an institute of Gullah Geechee art.

Pavilions house arts education programs rooted in preserving Gullah Geechee history and crafts through an artist-in-residence program. The pavilions and their programs allow current residents of the island to teach the history of their ancestors and their art while allowing artists from outside the island to participate and teach alongside them.

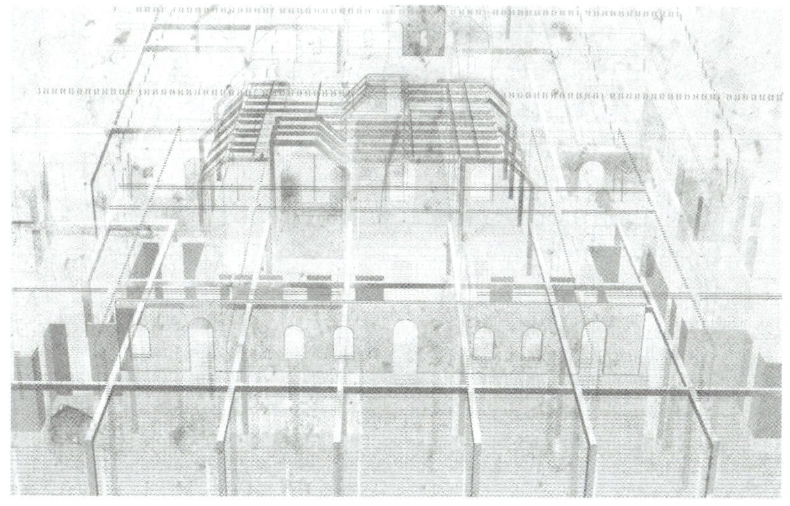

1 Tools for designing the project programs

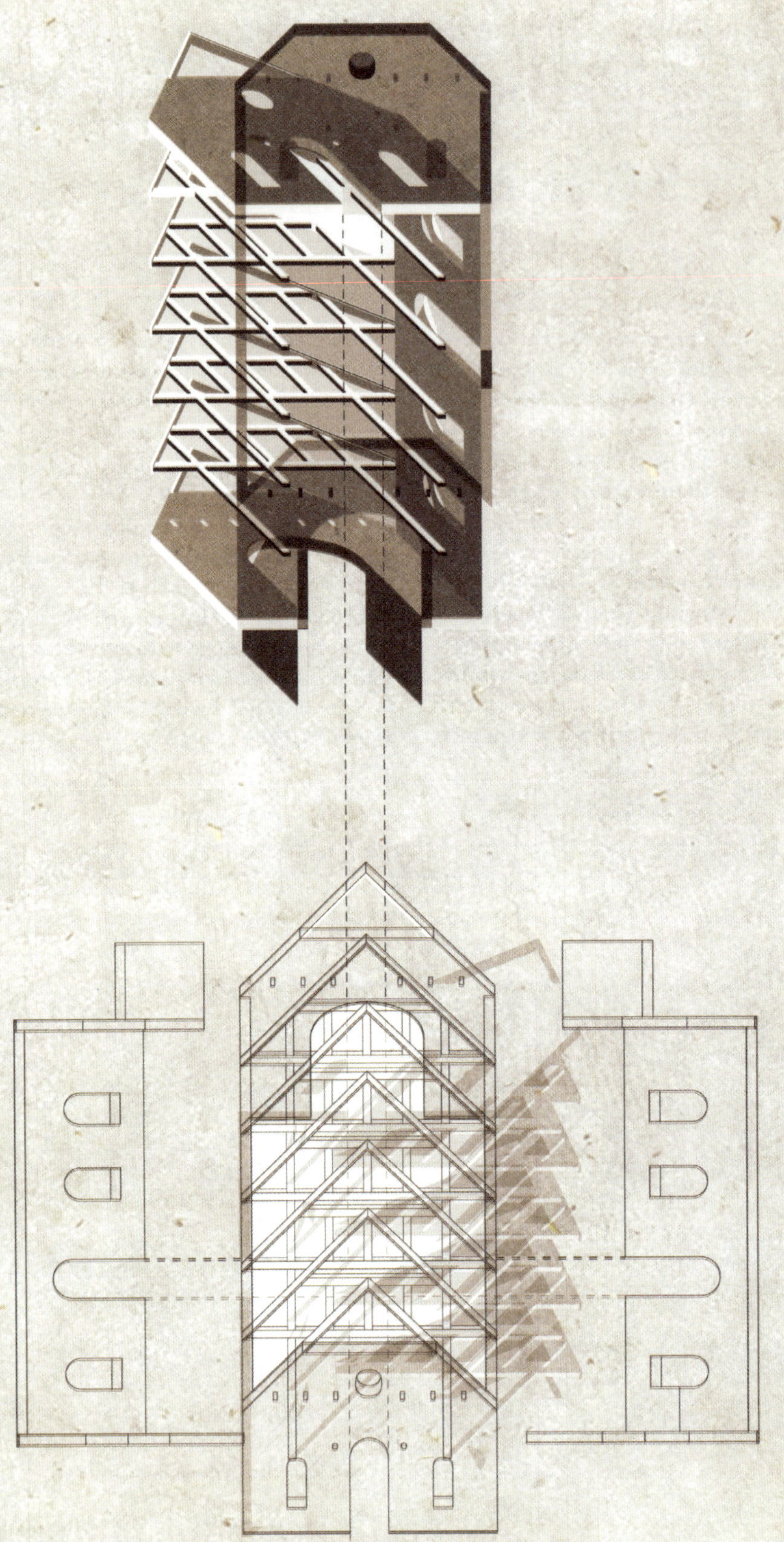
2

3

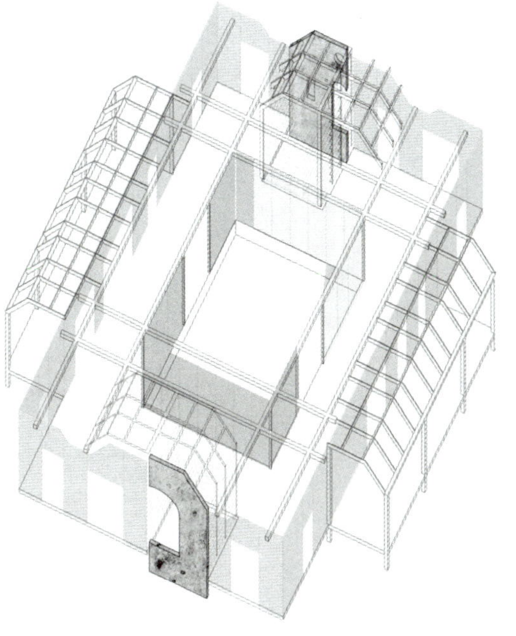

4

2 Diagrammatic drawings showing the materials of the Chapel of Ease under deconstruction and reconstruction

3 Pavilion for a writing program

4 Pavilion for sweetgrass basket-weaving studio and exhibition

5

7
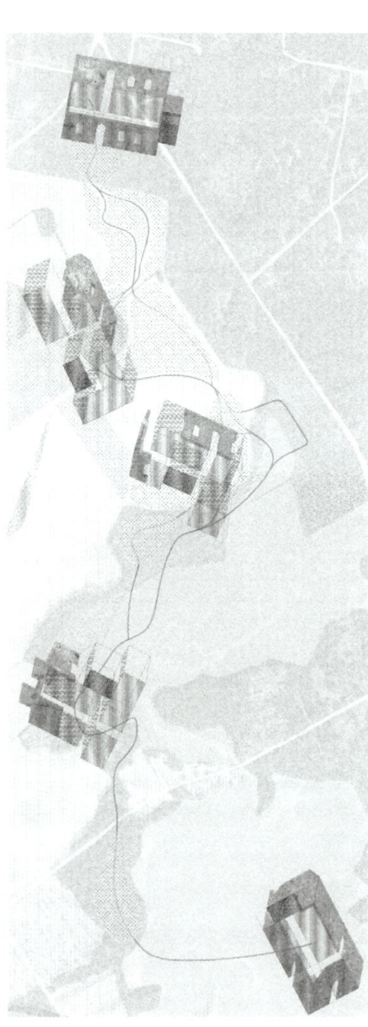

5 Section cut of the painting pavilion showcasing the art studios and an exhibition space

6 The painting pavilion's bar opens periodically onto courtyard gardens

7 To reflect the journey of the Gullah Geechee and their ancestors, the structure of the chapel ruin is dismantled and rebuilt on its new location. Core programs for the different centers

8 Painting pavilion

9 Current ruin of the St. Helena Parish Chapel of Ease in Frogmore, South Carolina

6

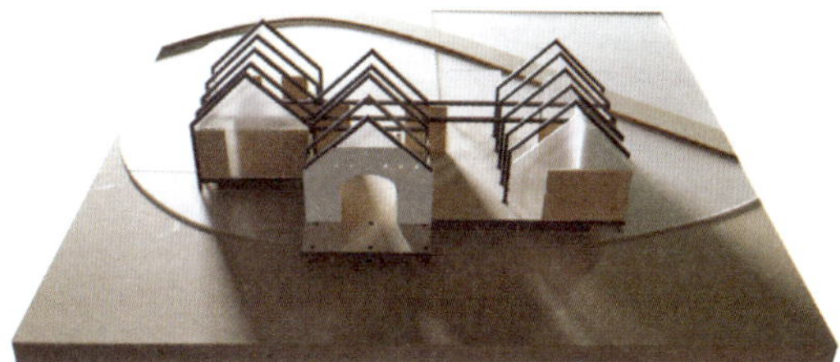

8

9

Hunter Hughes Monument and Museum

Located at the water's edge, the Old Exchange was once a symbol of prosperity for the city of Charleston. Over the years the edge of the city has been pushed out, and the memory of its role in the slave trade has been forgotten. Charleston was once one of the wealthiest cities in America. Its wealth was built on slavery and the rich agricultural soil that produced rice, or "Carolina Gold," and later cotton. From the beginning the eastern edge of Charleston was a large shipping area, where goods grown on area plantations were traded. This proposal aims to revive the Old Exchange as a destination for trade. Two parking lots currently separate the water's edge from the Exchange building, one private and the other for visitors. This proposal carves a tidal pool through the city right to the doorstep of the Exchange. It places the museum over the water as a symbol of the vessels that used to adorn the city's edge.

The museum entry dock becomes submerged during high tide and revealed during low tide. At the end of the walk you slip below the building and into the receiving hold, located under a vertical shaft that allows light in from above. At the end of the hold is an elevator that ascends to the second floor, with a view out to the sea, before entering the gallery through a series of heavy curtains. North-facing sawtooth forms inside the dimly lit gallery reference the sea and a sense of containment. The exit sequence is reached by ascending a narrow stair passage where the viewer is released from the dark containment of the gallery to access a clear view over the tidal pool and the Exchange building. The only sawtooth motif found to the south is located in the exit hold; it provides a symbolic connection between the ocean and the south and between the Exchange and the west.

1

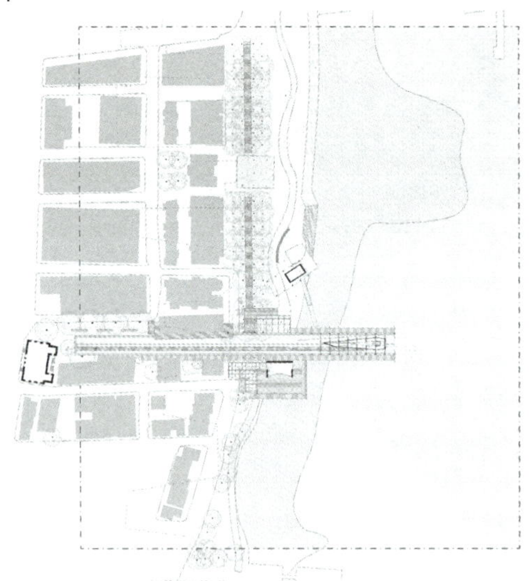

1 Entry to the museum limited by tidal fluctuations

2 View approaching the museum from tidal pool

2

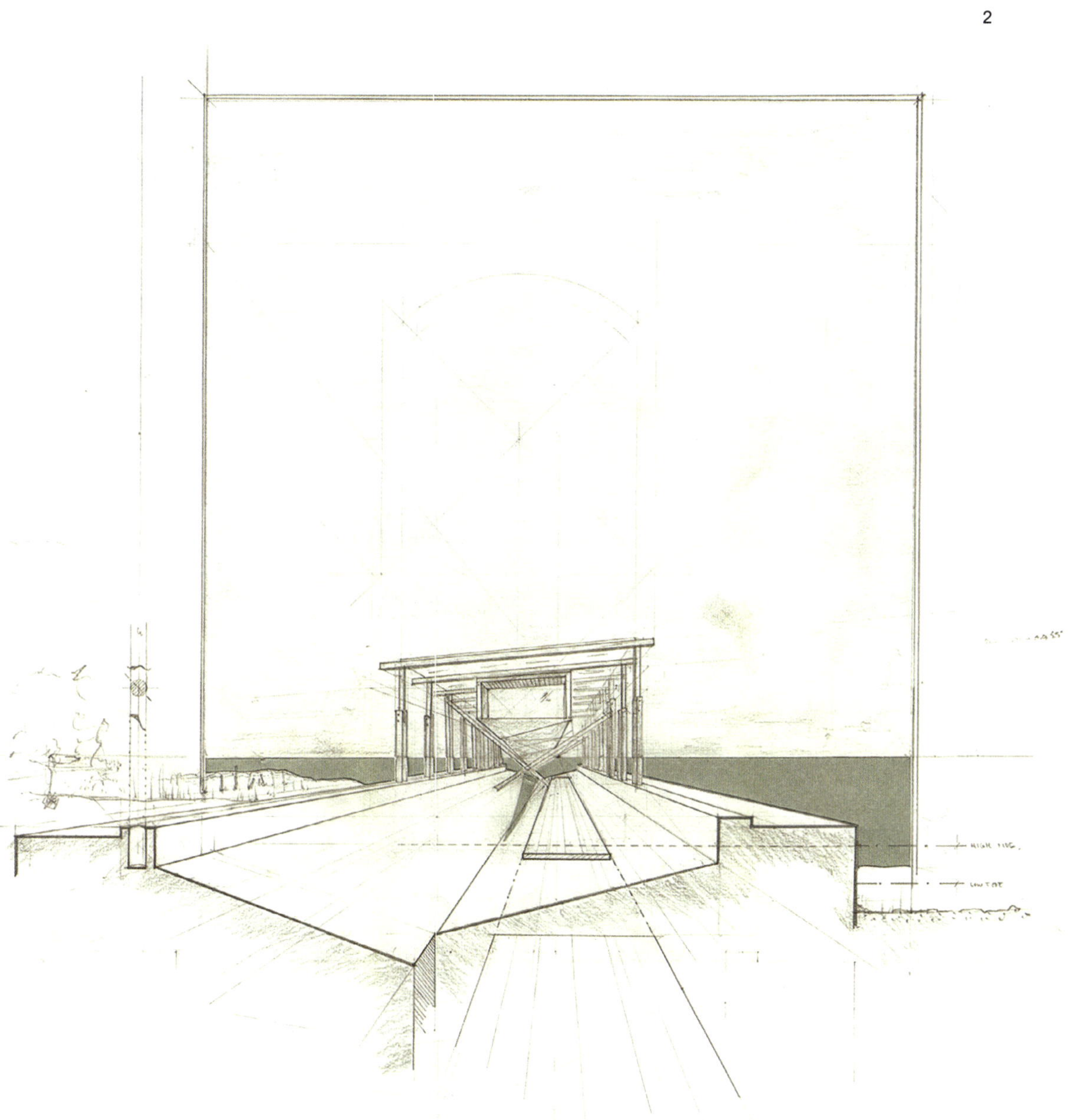

3

4

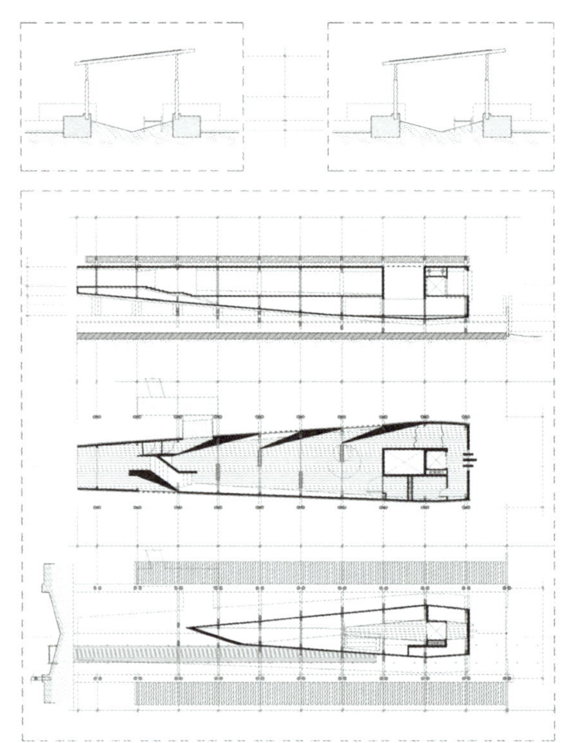

5

6

3 Remains contained within the water. This passage in Christine Sharpe's book The Wake talks about the custom of jettisoning slaves during the journey through the Middle Passage. Thus the water contains the memory and residue of the terrible acts of our ancestors in the slave trade. The concept of "the wake" became central to this investigation and remembering the history of this maritime city.

4 Sawtooth forms calibrated for light to animate museum interior

5 Final model

6 Although Charleston's history features significant locations in the surrounding Sea Islands, this project focused on the city peninsula, the first stop for many people at the docks. The wharfs at the eastern edge of the city saw a great amount of trade and commerce, all dependent on African labor.

7 Final model

Alexandra Thompson
High Ground

This project operates on a location rich with historical significance, particularly for the African-American community of its Charleston neighborhood. The site has cycled through several iterations in the past century alone: first as Hemlock Court, a group of houses owned by African-American residents, followed by DeReef Park, a pocket park beloved by the entire neighborhood. The block has great historical significance, with the Cannon Street Y, the oldest YMCA in the country serving African Americans; the United Order of Tents, a black women's benevolent society; Shiloh AME Church; the now demolished Simonton School; and the Brooks Motel.

This project aims to create a superimposed ground over the former park. Lifting the ground level will create space for a number of buildings in the park, which will be both park land and community center. The program of the community center will host institutions of African-American cultural production on the peninsula, including the Avery Center, Cannon Street Y, and Dart Library. The buildings physically join several of these institutions to create entry forecourts on three sides of the block. The light wells that dot the park echo the forms of the houses on Hemlock Court, appearing in the same proportion and rhythm. The raised earth of the park also addresses the problem of flooding with a surplus of pervious earth to absorb water and create an island of dry ground on the historic site. This island suggests a new typology for historic preservation in Charleston that creates higher ground to aid against flooding.

1

2

3

1 Final model

2 Community green space at the center of higher ground

3 The integration of existing and historical neighborhood conditions

4

4 Located between existing ground and a new ground plane, the buildings are lit from above and look outward.

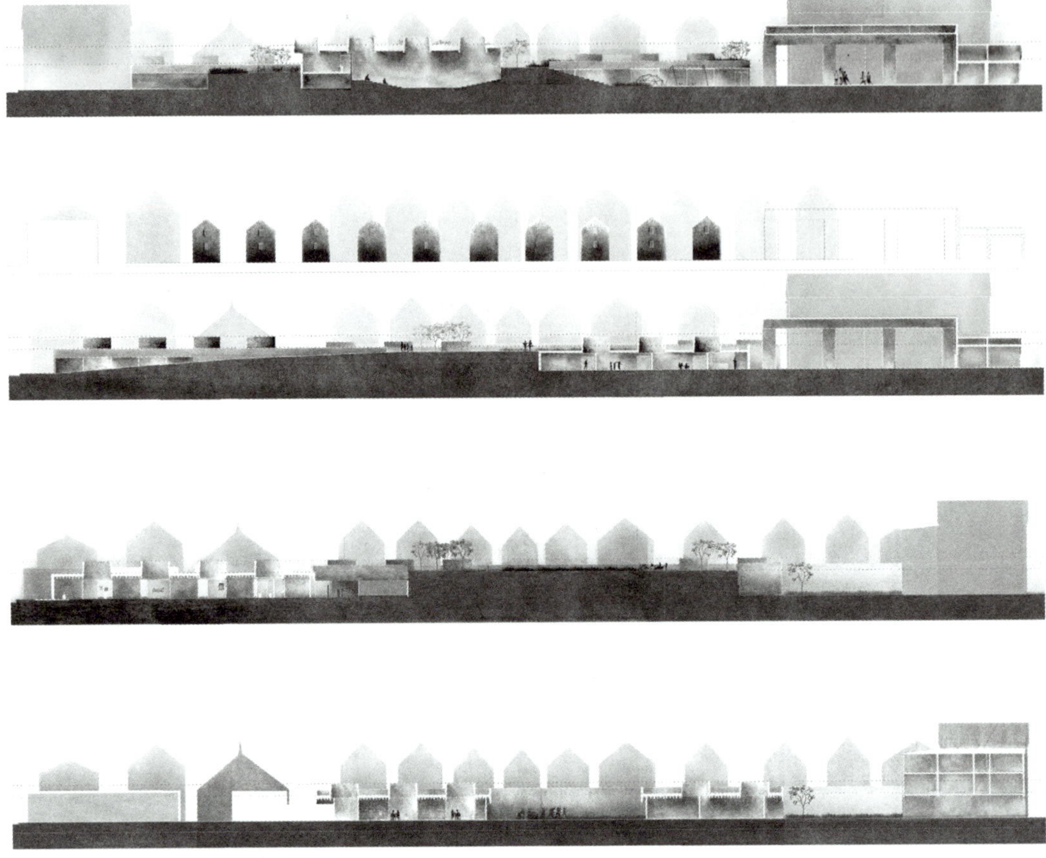

5

6

5 Rhythms of existing and historical buildings on the site that organize the section

6 Plan showing how the footprints of historical buildings are "ghosted" into the new complex

Pat Doty
Station Creek Landing

Beaufort, on St. Helena Island, has long been the cultural center of the community and is the last Sea Island that is still predominantly Gullah Geechee. It is also home to institutions and heritage celebrations that bring local and expatriate communities together. The site is on the southwestern shore of the island at Station Creek Landing—a concrete peninsula that juts out into the marshes and separates St. Helena from the barrier islands—with an existing boat launch and spectacular marsh views.

In recognition of the complex pressures and increasingly tenuous relationship between the Gullah Geechee and the institutions and traditions that have historically brought the community together, the program and architectural language play a role in fostering cultural continuation and economic independence. The proposed set of structures at Station Creek Landing aims to foster community cohesion in a time of turbulence and adaptation and to employ tourism to bring revenue to the community while avoiding cultural commodification.

The project focuses on a set of enclosed, semi-enclosed, and open rooms arranged toward different views of the marsh and for preferred lighting conditions given individual functions, and composed as a series of terraces given processional routes and natural light. Buildings devoted to farming and ecotourism (fishing, boat tours, and kayak rentals) are set near the base of the peninsula. After passing a thicket of newly planted live oaks surrounding these structures, one continues upward across three terraces, passing a bar and restaurant, a community kitchen, and a fishing pier to ultimately arrive at a multipurpose community building and a memorial porch. The Gullah Geechee people have passed down their history and traditions through conversation, and communal spaces like these are intended to support this practice. The terraces between the buildings serve as day-to-day community spaces, circulation, festival and performance venues, and market spaces. What is currently a massive concrete parking lot with prime views has become a green acropolis devoted to the Gullah Geechee community.

The buildings are arranged to favor a variance of light and shadow and to frame and highlight people. This approach manifests in several places, particularly in the initial approach, where an angled pair of buildings and a dense grouping of trees obscure lines of sight to the rest of the peninsula. A curved procession around the trees reveals an arrangement of angled planes, terrace benches, and clusters of vegetation forming a composition that climaxes through mid to late afternoon—a time when the complex would be in greatest use. The procession to the main community building proceeds upward from terrace to terrace at alternating angled openings in the vegetation. The upper terrace is given the greatest emphasis. The faster cadence of the terrace benches is intended to contrast the large blank planes of the community building. A small garden shed in front of the community kitchen is angled and faced with an open void to create a shaded pocket in direct sunlight. The overall intent is to elevate the buildings and the human form, and to celebrate the people and traditions of the Gullah Geechee community.

1

2

1 Midday section through community and meeting rooms. The space's elevated platform is free of adjacent walls and reached over a slot dividing the two halves of the building.

2 Plan of proposed development at Station Creek Landing, St. Helena Island

3 Late afternoon at the bar. An open circulation spine divides the bar and restaurant seating, creating a sequence of light and shadow.

4 Community room looking south-southeast. The multipurpose community room has an open view toward the marshes and, along with the semienclosed room immediately preceding it, is intended to be a new porch for the community.

3

4

5

6

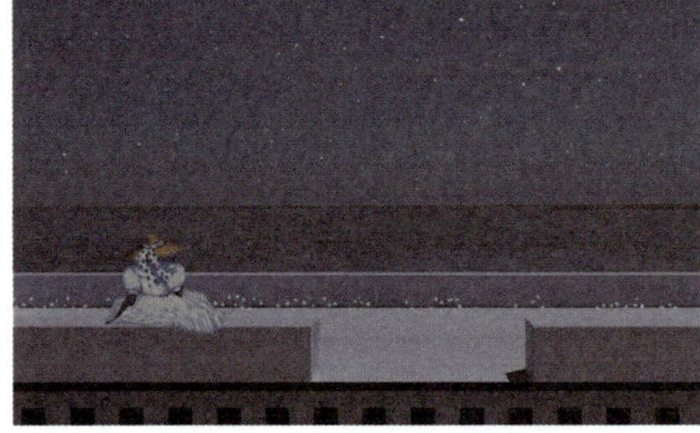

7

5 Community room, memorial porch, and fishing pier from harbor

6 Entrance procession east

7 Memorial porch. Dedicated to the victims of enslavement and continued racism, the porch is a negation of the community room, whereby the overall dimensions are in equal proportion to the room preceding it, rotated ninety degrees. The porch deck is quartz, considered a symbol of the human spirit and a channel for ancestral knowledge. The well-known Kalunga Line—the watery boundary dividing the worlds of the living and the dead often discussed in relation to the Middle Passage—is referenced by emphasizing horizontality through a full-length quartz wall and a preceding band of small holes cut into the stone to serve as flower vessels.

8

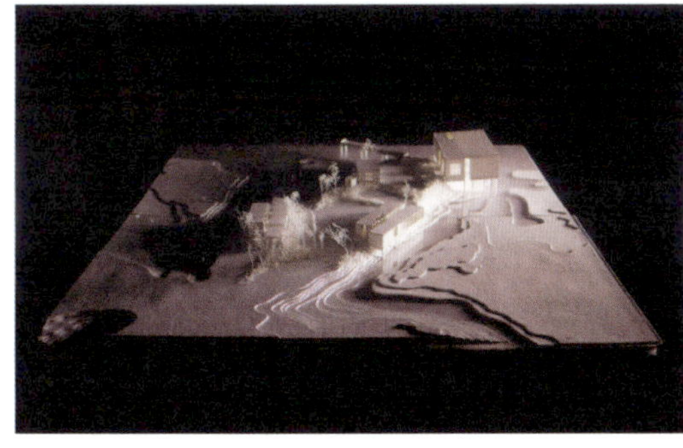

9

10

8–10 Final model

Claire Haugh and Caitlin Baida
A Living Memorial

How do you memorialize a culture that is threatened yet not extinct? These proposals explore the reconstruction of painful historical narratives in tourism and development projects formulated by the Gullah Geechee people. Implemented in Charleston (urban resolution) and St. Helena Island (site and architectural resolution), this strategy created a productive dialogue that reinforced essential aspects of Gullah Geechee culture throughout the Low Country.

The Living Memorial on St. Helena Island, situated on one of the last remaining shoreline parcels, is a collectively owned and publicly accessible ecofarm for tourism preserving traditional Gullah Geechee agricultural techniques. The project explores how ecotourism could sustain the self-sufficient Gullah Geechee way of life while immersing visitors in its rituals and a transient landscape of water, earth, and architecture. The program memorializes the culture's past and reawakens marginalized space by adapting to a changing present and uncertain future. The site plan references both the gridded parcels of land subdivided by the government for purchase by former slaves and the subsequent denial of that grid, by the Gullah Geechee, who have built homes according to the organic logic of community proxemics.

The project explores how urban-renewal infrastructure can be reimagined as a bike and pedestrian low-line reconnecting Charleston's disempowered north from a gentrifying south. The "island" of derelict land at the center of two raised highways is redeveloped into an urban wetland—a counterpart to the controversial Calhoun statue in Marion Square, where the proposed low-line terminates. A series of local businesses and incubators, constructed on vacant lots as additions to existing building stock, serve as sources of economic empowerment for Charleston's African-American community while acting as low-line gateways restitching the city together from east to west.

A community kitchen honors the tradition of Gullah Geechee community proxemics through its formal shift off axis from the memorialized grid, which references the government-imposed "heirs property" subdivision. The architecture appears alternately to float above or be embedded in the earth. Planted in an exterior skin, the primary floor plate allows space for earth and water to enter. Guests circulate through an elevated pantry and the interstitial space between the building's skin and program, subverting traditional notions of "service" and "served" imposed upon slave communities. Cabins organized into community clusters ground visitors and provide a vertical connection to the sky. Each cabin on the St. Helena Island ecofarm comprises a central "embedded" concrete block that acts as the structural base and is carved to provide space for activities such as sleeping and bathing. Surrounding this central core is a lightweight skin that "floats" above the landscape, continuing the themes of the kitchen. The visitor becomes "embedded" in the landscape by lying down in the recessed bed to look at stars through the skylight or view the landscape through the low panoramic window.

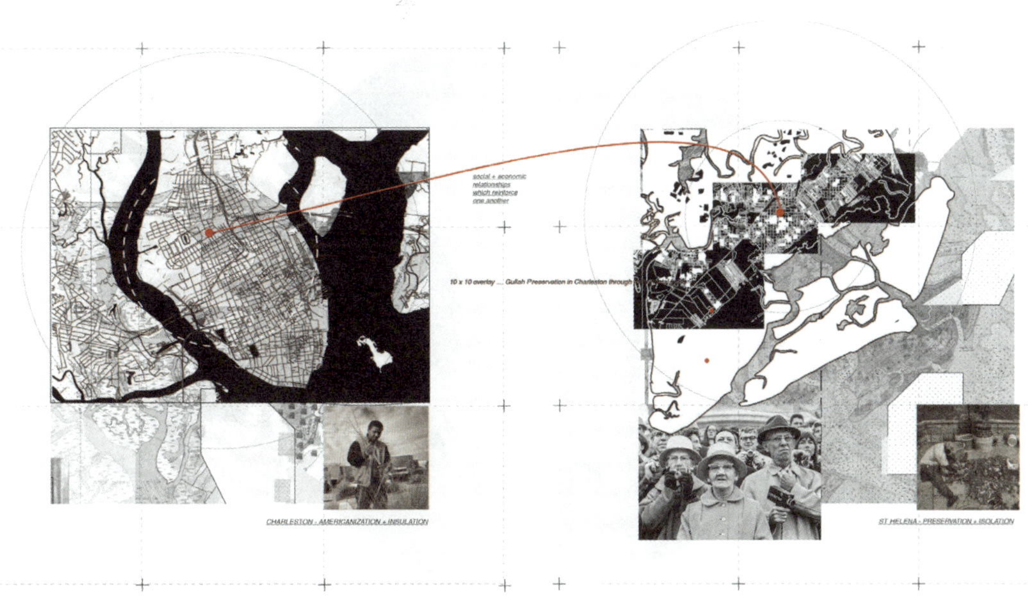

1

2

1 Conceptual diagram

2 Site model, Charleston's "low-line" interventions and bike path, designed to promote interaction between tourists and African-American residents

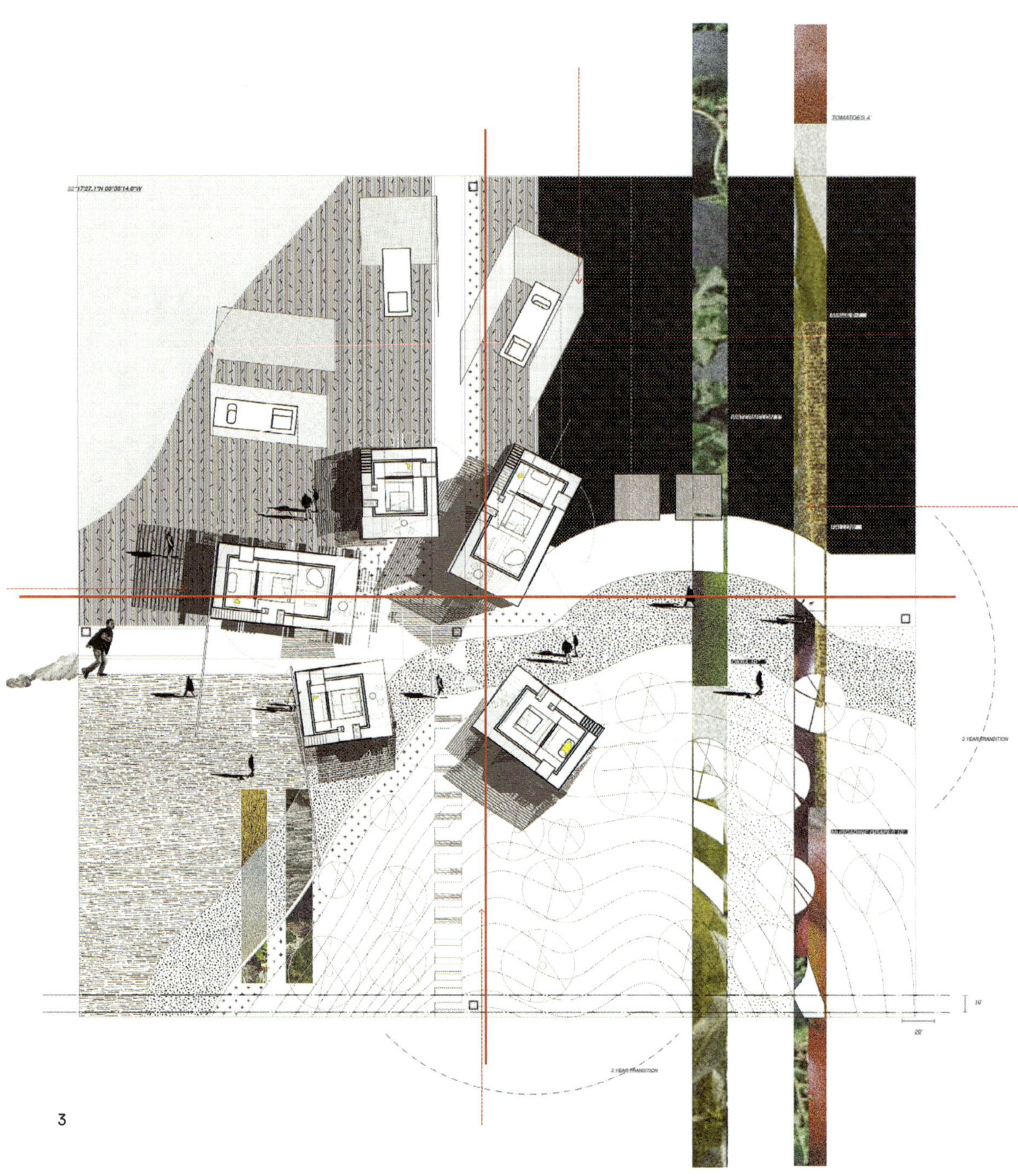

3

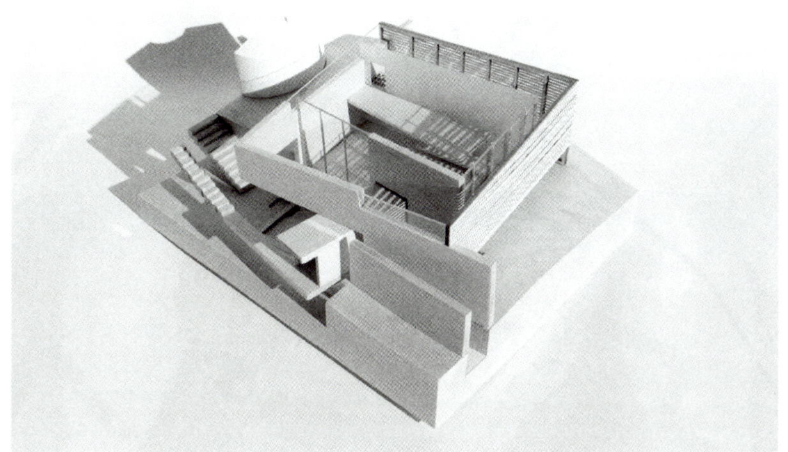

4

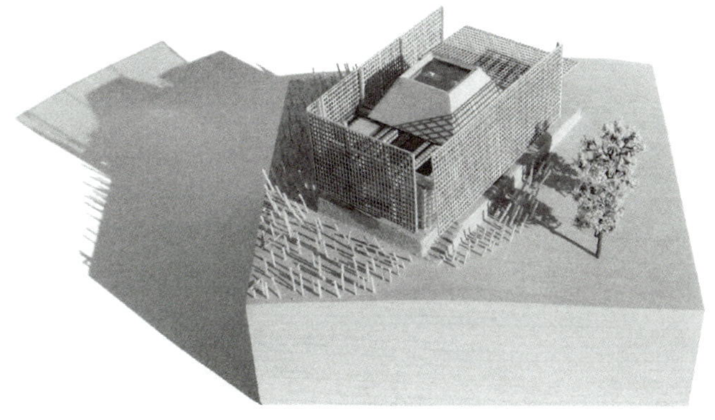

5

3 Plan for a cluster of cabins on St. Helena Island

4 Axonometric view, St. Helena Island community kitchen model

5 Model, St. Helena Island cabin

6

7

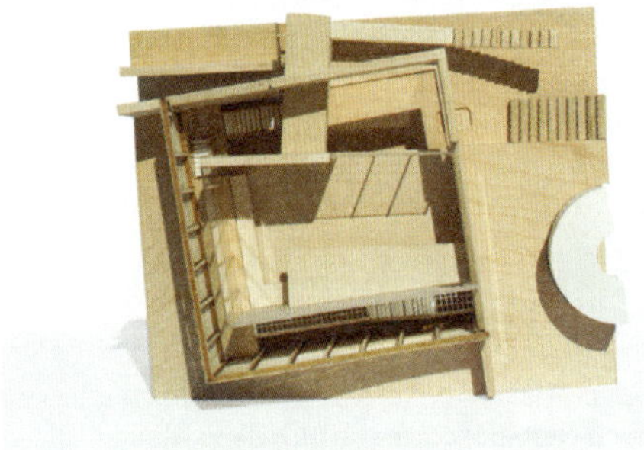

8

6 Vacant lots identified as potential locations for local businesses and incubators

7 Plan view, St. Helena Island community kitchen model

8 Model, St. Helena Island cabin

Image credits

Scott Ruff: 4-5, 6, 7, 9

M.S. Clarke. "The Economy of South Carolina," The Crucial Decade: 1780s, December 6, 2012: 12

Wikimedia Commons: 14

Megan Royster: 27, 33, 34, 35, 36

Jonathan Molloy & Samuels Zeif: 29, 38, 39, 40-41 (top), 41 (bottom)

Pierre Thach: 42, 43, 44-45 , 46

Abena Bonna: 28, 47, 48, 49, 50, 51

Hunter Hughes: 19, 52, 53, 54, 55, 56-57

Alexandra Thompson: 58, 59, 60-61, 62

Pat Doty: 64, 65, 66, 67

Claire Haugh & Caitlin Baiada: 20-21, 22, 23, 25, 26, 69, 70, 71, 72

Florencia Pita and
Jackilin Hah Bloom

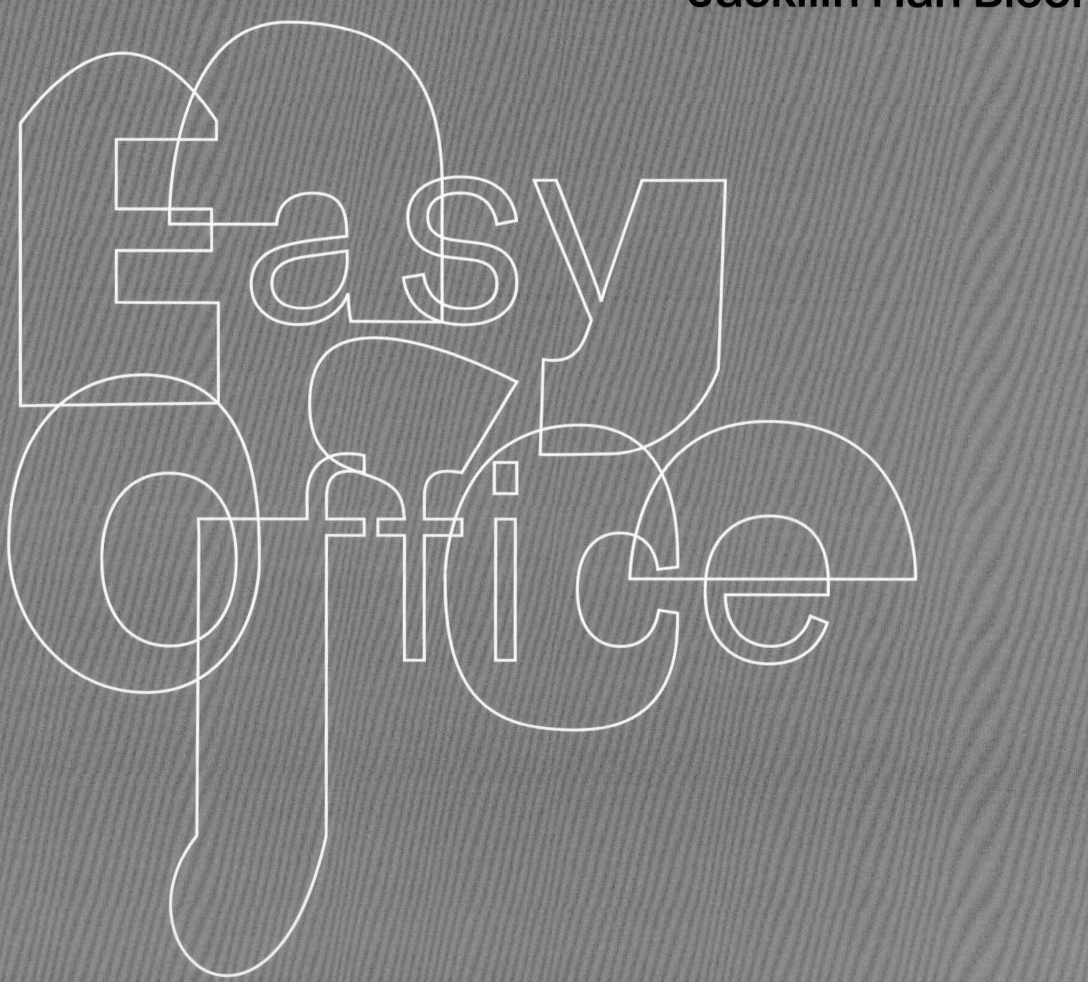

Contents

with
Nina Rappaport, Florencia Pita,
and
Jackilin Hah Bloom

NINA RAPPAPORT
Your collaborative work is very speculative yet also very rigorous, formal, graphic, and focused on lines and curves as well as ideas of tracing and layering. How does your work process inspire and influence your forms? What is your interest in the figurative?

FLORENCIA PITA
We aim to work on both ideas and buildings. We are trying to be very specific about how we work on every project and assume that they will get built. We have a focus on the figurative curve, and we use it in design and certain matters of form.

JACKILIN HAH BLOOM
When we started working together, the figurative curve was a generative point of departure to establishing and processing our own thinking and sensibilities of figure and form.

NR

How did you decide to leave Greg Lynn's office, and what was it like starting to collaborate together?

FP

I was at Greg's for five years and Jacki was there about ten. We developed shared sensibilities and ideas while we were there. Our connection to Greg's work may not be readily apparent, but there are a lot of things in our work that he initiated. Greg is a real inventor. We tried to narrow down the problems we wanted to work on and really question them.

NR

One focus of your work is color, which is rare among architects these days. How did you rediscover color as an essential element of architecture and extract ideas of color theory from Josef Albers to Pantone and Pop Art?

FP

Indeed when we started there was not much emphasis on color; there was a lot of white and black with some splashes of paint. Now, at least in academia, we see the whole world of color. We're art junkies and feel a connection with multigenerational artists who have similar conflicts with the relationship between the analog and the digital. Art owns color much more than architecture, so we look at how contemporary artists deal with materials, patterns, color, texture, and so on. In a way we find or match the effect within architecture. We look at color as a way to challenge materials, as artists did in the 1960s and '70s.

NR

Some of your form-and-color combinations are Post-Modern, and some of your formal characteristics are close to the work of Robert Venturi and Charles Moore but distinct from your digital approach. The curves in your Ikea chair project, for example, are reminiscent of Venturi's furniture, and your tracing projects recall his Benjamin Franklin house, in Philadelphia. Do you place your work within the trajectory of Post-Modernism or contemporary ideas such as the projects of FAT as well as the digital?

JHB

There is definitely a visual alignment, but our process is more recursive: although there's a lot of sampling at the beginning, it is very disciplined and selective. The design will get reconfigured in several steps. It is almost impossible to trace back where the original curves or geometries begin.

I would say it is the difference between pure image making and symbol making. It's more about producing multiple readings of the origins of these geometries.

FP

Of course we look at that work. The issue of graphics, from *Learning from Las Vegas* to *Complexity and Contradiction*, is important to us. Although we start with lines that form a signature, we end up with lines that are more abstract. We question the curves themselves. In the New Zocalo, for the Venice Biennale, the references start to dissolve and the curve takes on a new form.

NR

You could say that your work is more about process than that of the Post-Modernists: you are finding form through your process, not the other way around.

JHB

I think that's a good way to put it.

NR

How do you form the rules, or rigor, around your design of curves?

JHB

We look closely at the specifics of each project. Proportion, composition, and scale are all issues we consider, and it's important that the curves and geometries establish a new datum or reference to dictate scale, proportion, and space.

NR

Do you know in advance what the results will be like?

JHB

Usually we start off not knowing. We go back and forth between form finding and making, and establish a project's overall composition and scale based on an instance of that process. In our competition entry for the Harvey Milk Plaza, called "Shaped Plaza," in addition to designing a color-infused flat ground surface we outlined a space-frame around the plaza that was generated from the scale of the surrounding buildings and contextual datum lines.

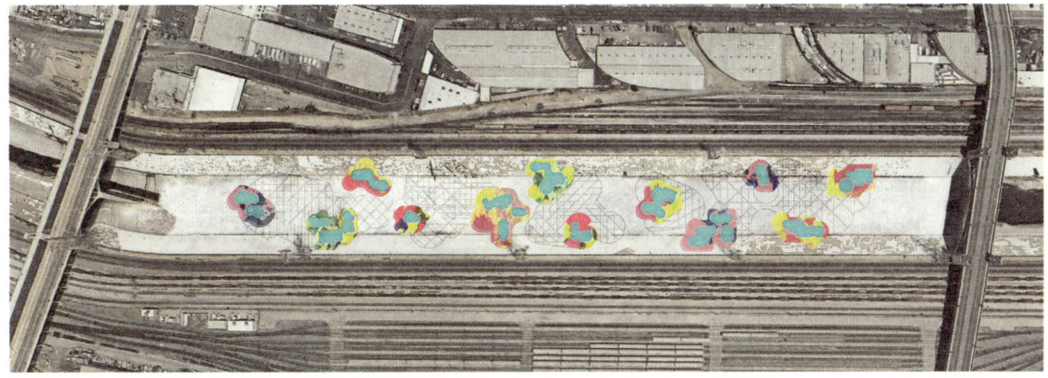

Pita and Bloom, Flat Pools: view between 6th Street and 4th Street bridges, speculative project for the LA River, 2017

Pita and Bloom, La Medianera: prototype of a rural low-income house in Mexico, 2017

FP

Similarly, in the 2016 Venice Biennale project there's a blur between what the graphic is doing with color and texture, what the volumes are doing in terms of mass, and what the lines are doing. We discovered that we could have mass, flatness, and the in-between, which is this lattice or curve. It is a space between the public and the private realms of a building. We envisioned the color to be a combination of nature and natural building material.

NR

How do you integrate the program or public use into this rigorous design method for a public space?

FP

We have participated in three design competitions where we investigate how art can engage public space. We don't believe programming necessarily activates public space, but architectural elements can transform the idea of it. We are working on "Flat Pools," a project for the Los Angeles river embankment that might become a commission to simply paint the riverbed, but even that can transform the infrastructure. Color has the power to engage open space.

NR

Your mural at the Princeton School of Architecture is interesting because of its animated vertical surface. You have used recognizable objects to create an unusual spatial depth. What was your approach to the project?

JHB

We designed many iterations of that image, from very abstract and unrecognizable to a return to the found imagery. At first we thought we were going to redesign the atrium by ARO and project the image of the new design on the building. But with a flat two-dimensional image there was a problem depicting a building on glass as well as conveying geometry and curves that would allow you to read between building and image. We created a synchronous collage of images in a background that would recede at night to epitomize the activity within the building because the image needed to remain as an image and not as a depiction or drawing of another building.

FP

In many projects we start with something very clear, like the form of a house, the outline of a caricature, or the curve of a piece of furniture. For the Princeton installation we combined familiar imagery with abstracted curves

Pita and Bloom, The New Zocalo: model, project for *The Architectural Imagination*, at the 15th Venice Architecture Biennale, 2016

and a single color. We are interested in a collage technique similar to the way Max Ernst sampled different things—a fish, a woman, wallpaper—in which the subjects are autonomous but embedded in each other, becoming more abstract through a process of drawing and redrawing. At Princeton you have clear references to the readymade and the abstraction of the curves. They're flat but tectonic, instead of being outlines. If you look at the images at night, they recede and you're left with only the lines.

NR

What you are describing is very nuanced and layered. I was amused by your 2014 MoMA PS1 installation entry, in which you used the signature and cartoon characters of the Macy's Day Parade balloons as the starting point. Was it because you liked the figures, the curves, the randomness, or the actual characters?

JHB

When we were told we were one of the finalists for PS1, at the end of the year, there were a lot of parades. The playfulness of the Macy's Thanksgiving Day Parade balloons, and their shadows projected onto buildings nearby, was really interesting to us. It helped generate the figures and forms,

Pita and Bloom, Signature: installation at the Princeton School of Architecture, 2016

and the sampling of those curves developed a whole series of digitally modeled balloons.

FP

This is one of the first projects where the lines separate from the surfaces. For us it is a discovery at the building scale. We were interested in the colors and the familiarity of some of the images that are maintained while others are abstracted. The discovery of this project was that we could work from 2-D to 3-D and back and forth. It was also economic because we had to build a sample, and the project relates to the idea of the balloon frame as a volume. Through the economy of reducing things to planes you have volume and lines, and by isolating the variables we combined them as a new collage.

NR

What has been the principal challenge in the INFONAVIT housing project in Mexico, and how is it important to your practice, aside from the fact that it will actually be built?

JHB

The challenge was to establish a design identity in a project that has a very, very low budget. But it's been surprisingly easy with the use of color as the material intervention in this project. INFONAVIT is going to build a prototype of this house, along with thirty or so others. They will be model homes. People will walk through them and select their favorite from a variety of designs by international architects.

NR

Teaching has been a significant part of your work. Do you present your own method of working or simply teach the fundamentals? What do you want your students to learn?

FP

Teaching provides us fertile ground for research. We teach elements isolated from what we do—for example, ways to look at and work with textures and models. We never do the same thing; teaching is about discovery for both the students and us.

JHB

I typically teach undergraduate core studios. When we teach together we try to convey an attitude about design and to liberate the students' approach to color and form. Color is not always seen as something indexical, and form is not always seen as an object's complete shape.

NR

How do you evaluate your work when it is speculative? And how do you reinterpret it or move into another area of exploration?

FP

Through teaching and lecturing we can think about the work and use it as an opportunity to uncover new territory.

This discussion was published
in the Spring 2018 issue of *Constructs.*

Easy Office

"What is so remarkable is the near total disengagement from signification of any kind. Such a condition is immensely difficult to achieve; mere abstraction does not begin to approach it."

—Robin Evans, 1984

The short film *Brillo Box (3¢ Off)* shows how the eponymous sculpture by Andy Warhol was purchased for $1,000 in 1969 and sat in a modest collector's home for only a few years before it was sold at a Christie's auction for close to $3 million. While the film primarily tells the story of the collector's family, it also documents Warhol's impact on the era's art consumerism. After the extraordinary Christie's sale, a journalist asks the artist why he turned an everyday item into sculpture. Warhol responds with his signature cool and casual indifference: "Because it's easy to do."[1] Closer evaluation elicits other questions: What did Warhol mean by "easy"? Was he referring to how advances in printmaking and fabrication allowed for the ease in reproducing Brillo boxes? Perhaps he was commenting on the signification of the Brillo graphics and the irony of commercial packaging being pushed as high art?

All of this could not be recontextualized for exhibit and appropriated as high art without the particular alignment of social, economic, and cultural forces of the era. In the case of this specific *Brillo Box*, designated as an artwork, it amounted to a massive auction sale.[2] There may be no equivalent of this kind of "easy" in architecture, but our discipline has a profound capacity to generate new ideas by looking at what is sometimes suppressed in popular culture. So we peeled back the irony behind *Brillo Box* and interpreted Warhol's remark as facetious—"easy" actually referred to the more difficult and rigorous design process of copying consumer brand logos through artistic mediums.

For our Yale studio we experimented with ways of generating new spatial, formal, material, and narrative ideas through creative processes that start with everyday objects. We looked closely at procedures of making, starting with the work of artist Rachel Whiteread. Like Warhol, she starts with an everyday or mundane object—a staircase, a bookshelf, an old shoe. However, rather than simply appropriating a recognizable thing, Whiteread undoes the aesthetic conditions of the original by foregrounding the distinct ways in which her work is made. Her installation *Embankment* (2005–6) poses a counterpoint to Warhol's stack of Brillo boxes with seemingly blank boxes that are

actually casts of the interior volumes of cardboard boxes.[3] The artwork calls attention to ways of manipulating space and scale and of disengaging with any signification while producing interpretations in arrangement and materiality. As art historian and critic James Lawrence states: "There is a heuristic sense of assembly, the feeling that these sculptures grew into themselves instead of emerging fully formed. As Whiteread works on the sculptures, she selects from an inventory of cast elements, often stacked on a trolley that she moves around the studio while she works. The resulting sculptures evince their particular

OPPOSITE: *Brillo Box*. 1964. Synthetic polymer paint and screenprint ink on wood. overall: 17 in. x 17 in. x 14 in. Andy Warhol (1928-1987) © Copyright. Courtesy Davis Museum at Wellesley College / Art Resource, NY

ABOVE: Clip from *Brillo Box (3¢ Off)*, directed by Lisanne Skyler, documentary, HBO, 2016

histories of selection and assembly. Each is a clear record of the decisions, acts, and judgments that guided its construction."[4] Whiteread's sculptures resonate even more with architecture when they take on the scale of monuments, houses, or stairs. Our interest in her work lies primarily in the accumulation of unforeseen opportunities that emerge in the recursive techniques behind the creation of her sculptures.

While there is much to mine from Whiteread's practices, in the Yale studio we focused on three procedures—collecting,

Rachel Whiteread, *Untitled (Twenty-Five Spaces)*, 1995, resin (twenty-five units), Private collection. © Rachel Whiteread. From the exhibition September 16, 2018 - January 13, 2019, National Gallery of Art, Washington, D.C.

collage, and casting. For the artist, accumulating a lot of stuff allows for a playful and uninhibited way to start working. Collecting can be defined by the hunt, not just by the objects obtained, therefore not limiting the act to a set of objectives or qualities. Walter Benjamin articulates this in his essay on collecting books: "What I am really concerned with is giving you some insight into the relationship of a book collector to his possessions, into collecting rather than a collection. If I do this by elaborating on the various ways of acquiring books, this is something entirely arbitrary. This or any other procedure is merely a dam against the spring tide of memories which surges toward any collector as he contemplates his possessions."[5]

Specific sensibilities may be evident in a collection, but the modes of looking at and curating objects reveal the collector's taste and set up parameters for authorship when the collection is deployed through a design process. Once a collection is amassed its contents are run through the medium of collage, a compositional technique that involves cutting and pasting items to produce a new whole or hybrid image. The medium's power lies in the unexpected entirety of the collage, which becomes a new independent image or object in which signifiers are depleted through fragmentation and juxtaposition. Collages can be fixed or have endless combinations. Most collages are made up of a combination of two- and three-dimensional images on a flat surface delineating where a figure or outline begins and ends.

In the studio students worked on two- and three-dimensional forms of collage, the latter through the assemblage and vacuum forming of full-scale objects. The collages steered most of the projects through either the formal articulation that emerged in the process or the ways in which they produced material grafts. The collaged results were then translated into programmatic and spatial scenarios and narratives. The third procedure introduced casting to the Yale students. Casting involves inversion, doubling, mirroring, and the filling of voids. The cast is a conversion of an object into a new and different version of itself where its material and textural characteristics take on new constructive purposes. "Whiteread's sculptures can dispense with the constructive order of armatures and facades because the casts are simultaneously internal and external. That, perhaps, is the primary attribute of her inside-out objects, and it explains why they seem to contradict what we understand about the way objects appear in space. By reconfiguring the relationship between armature and visible surface, Whiteread's casts expose practical characteristics to the process of aesthetic judgment. When the interior of a box is translated into a cast, for example, it must in turn be assessed in a different language. Stripped of the qualities that made them useful as containers, Whiteread's boxes are transformed from functional tools into aesthetic objects."[6] All three procedures performed by the students enabled an exploratory and recursive workflow that produced combinations of distinct elements through both two-dimensional collage imaging and three-dimensional collage modeling. These images informed the making and exploration of three-dimensional forms and conditions while suggesting intermediate 2.5-dimension possibilities.

While exploring these creative procedures, the students researched and considered ideas of work and the workplace. The project "Easy Office" looked closely at the history of the office and its relationship to the contemporary workplace focusing on one main question: What is the role of architecture in the design of an office space? Beyond that they investigated what dictates the notion of a "creative office." Students visited the studio site, an area of Los Angeles that has transformed in the last twenty years from a light industrial zone to one populated with creative office spaces, called the Hayden Tract of Culver City.

Since office interiors are dominated by program organization and office furniture, the students made a case for architectural thinking and design within this territory. The process involved rigorous work in analog making before digital modeling, followed by making again from the digital models. Translation from analog to digital was a crucial focus of the studio. Multiple analog techniques were explored and followed up with homologous digital techniques. Transitioning between these two realms allowed students to investigate the advantages each tool offered as well as prospects for novel translation and development of the project at various stages. Although the function of office space was not the generative principle for each project, the students' final schemes displayed varied and imaginative narratives of the workplace based on the unexpected configurations of space, form, and materiality derived from the effects and artifacts that emerged in the design process. These narratives presented ad hoc ways of using space and articulating work-space scenarios.

Although process-based pedagogy is not new territory, it seems appropriate now more than ever to continue to foster new ways of observing, making, drawing, and building architecture in a context that is not only postdigital but also hyperdigital. Advancements in digital design and fabrication offer ease in the output of highly calibrated architectural forms and provocative representations. The availability of content and information offers easily accessible sources of precedents to study and reiterate. Converting intuition, creativity, and sensibility into a more authored intelligence, however, is where architecture can continue to offer new insights.

1 Clip from *Brillo Box (3¢ Off)*, directed by Lisanne Skyler, documentary, HBO, 2016.

2 The parents of Lisanne Skyler, director of *Brillo Box (3¢ Off)*, bought a 1963 Brillo Box in 1969 for $1,000 and had Andy Warhol sign it. They sold it after two years. Forty years later it sold at a Christie's auction for $3 million.

3 *Embankment* was an installation by Rachel Whiteread of thousands of blank translucent polyethylene boxes in the Turbine Hall of the Tate Modern, in London.

4 James Lawrence, *Rachel Whiteread* (New York: Gagosian Gallery, 2008), 8.

5 Walter Benjamin, *Illuminations* (New York: Houghton Mifflin Harcourt, 2019), 59–60.

6 James Lawrence, *Rachel Whiteread* (New York: Gagosian Gallery, 2008), 13.

Studio Brief

What is the role of architecture in office design? Our Yale studio considered this question in the transformation of an industrial warehouse building into an "Easy Office." The term *easy office* is a paradox. On one hand, it refers to the underlying disciplinary aim of the studio: architecture that does not merely rely on the easy signification of found objects but looks for new formal, spatial, and material possibilities through rigorous, difficult, and creative processes of design. It also implies that the typology of the office as a place of work involving various forms of labor has evolved in many ways to make productivity easier, or at least seem easier. Through research on the history of office space—from the pretechnological autonomous cubicle layout to the hypertechnological, interactive, and open work environment and the current assortment of coworking and shared spaces—we know that storefront systems and café-like amenities dominate office interiors today. Offices also reflect the forces that command work: interaction, privacy, and creativity. Each student proposed innovative office narratives formulated through the serendipitous possibilities of material, form, and space that emerged from three heuristic procedures: collect, collage, and cast. The students operated through these procedures, at first linearly and then through a recursive design process that jumped between 2-D drawings and 3-D models and between analog and digital techniques. The residue of each step impacted an architectural assemblage that offered new narratives for office design.

1: Collect

We began the semester by asking students to "go shopping" for everyday items to start a collection. Students sourced their collections from Staples, Home Depot, Ikea, and dollar stores. The prompt was to look for banal, everyday office items and other objects they were drawn to arbitrarily. As the practice of collecting takes time and involves looking closely at things, coveting and then hunting down a desired item, this first exercise urged the students to be impulsive and find affinities between objects instantly rather than overthink what they were obtaining. Once the shopping was complete, they took stock of their items to determine what might be inferred from the collections. Students photographed each object and considered the photographs in terms of elevation, perspective, lighting, and shadow. The images were to be cropped, scaled, filtered, and aligned or misaligned deliberately. These photographic series became curated compilations exhibiting the students' emerging sensibilities. The more cohesive, specific, and obsessive the collection, the better it was read and observed.

2: Collage

The collections of "stuff" were then grouped as an ensemble through methods of collage (2-D) and vacuum forming (3-D). The collages were individually printed images hand cut and pasted onto Alvin Quadrille 17-by-22-inch gridded paper. Students were asked to consider the space of the gridded paper as a canvas in which the scale, alignment, overlaps, and crops of each object in relation to another would play on juxtapositions or similarities. Each student produced a 3-D version of the collage—an assemblage of the physical objects. Although the scale and materiality of the objects could not be manipulated in the same way as the images, different relationships between objects were examined while producing the assemblage. These assemblages were photographed and then vacuum formed in white styrene, producing abstracted 3-D models of the 2-D collages, with crude and unpredictable outcomes. Some objects were identifiable beneath the sheath of white plastic; in those that lacked distinction, imprints of textures and thicknesses of objects emerged. Students were asked to photograph their white vacuum forms and use the photographs as underlays to produce their first line drawings. They essentially read this photographic image of an abstracted vacuum-form model and translated it through architectural notations of line thickness and styles, color, hatches, and fill. These drawings accumulated more information in the process and characterized conditions such as figural voids, aggregation of disparate parts, superpositioning of textures, and so on. Each of these features was to be translated into office organization, space, and program.

3: Cast

Instead of digitally scanning or modeling found objects that had been assembled and vacuum-sealed together, students cast their forms in plaster. They used the vacuum forms as molds to produce rigid imprints of the idiosyncrasies that emerged from the collaged objects. The students employed these casts to produce not only a physical model of combined objects but also tactile reliefs of textures and material surface residues. They also tested color pigments at this stage.

4: Site

An architect who worked with Eric Owen Moss Architects, gave the students a tour of the Hayden Tract of Culver City Los Angeles, for which the firm was involved in many projects. We had asked the students to select an existing warehouse building on the site by looking at satellite photos so that while there they could take photographs of its exterior and context. Their visit included tours of Morphosis, Emerson College Los Angeles Center, Disney Concert

Hall, the Broad Art Museum, the Eames House, and a few creative and tech office spaces. A tour of Google's campus in Venice—including the old Chiat/Day Building, designed by Frank Gehry—allowed students to see how the company's organization responded to an existing "collage" of spatial conditions. As part of their midterm the students presented their collections and collages to a group of jurors at SCI-Arc.

5: Representation
The Developed Surface

The technique for representing the office projects was the "developed surface," as defined by Robin Evans. Just as the gridded paper was used as a substratum for the collage, the developed-surface drawing became a canvas for the project where a plan or top view is located centrally with unfolded interior elevations at each edge. This allowed for the conflation of lines, collage fragments, and photographs of casts to produce descriptions of space, form, and organization. The final models reflected these drawings in three dimensions, notably where projects had hinged walls that could fold down flat and contained the multiple mediums used throughout the semester—casts, vacuum forms, images, 3-D prints, and laser cuts.

Bibliography

Brillo Box (3¢ Off). Directed by Lisanne Skyler. HBO, 2016.

Robin Evans, "In Front of Lines That Leave Nothing Behind" (1984), in *Architecture Theory since 1968*, ed. K. Michael Hays (Cambridge, Massachusetts: MIT Press, 1998), 482–89.

Robin Evans, "The Developed Surface: An Inquiry into the Brief Life of an Eighteenth-Century Drawing Technique," in *Translations from Building to Drawing* (Cambridge, Massachusetts: MIT Press, 1996), 195–231.

Imagine ... Rachel Whiteread: Ghosts in the Room. Directed by Morag Tinto. BBC, 2017.

Sylvia Lavin, "Architecture in Extremis," *Log 22: The Absurd*, ed. Michael Meredith (London: Architectural Association, 2014).

Charlotte Mullins, "Architectonic Ghosts: House 1993," in *Rachel Whiteread* (New York: Anyone Corporation, 2011), 39–50.

Sianne Ngai, "The Cuteness of the Avant-Garde," in *Our Aesthetic Categories* (Cambridge, Massachusetts: Harvard University Press, 2012), 53–109.

Playtime. Directed by Jacques Tati, 1967.

R. E. Somol and Sarah Whiting, "Notes on the Doppler Effect and Other Moods of Modernism," *Perspecta 33: Mining Autonomy* (Cambridge, Massachusetts: MIT Press, 2002).

Robert Venturi, "The Inside and the Outside," in *Complexity and Contradiction in Architecture* (New York: Museum of Modern Art, 1977), 70–87.

Student work

Student work

Sharmin Bhagwagar
Disparate Organs

What began as an exercise in understanding the spatial and tactile qualities of everyday objects engendered a serious reconsideration of the warehouse type of creative office. The office space is viewed programmatically as an open landscape of follies and individual clusters with distinct identities that incorporate certain memories of the original warehouse. As the organization begins to expand its boundaries, porosity increases and eventually the boundaries cease to exist, the memory of the original warehouse remaining only in the materiality of the clusters. The project culminated in a physical model expressing the diverse spatial conditions in a state of transition between the original warehouse building and the new clusters.

1

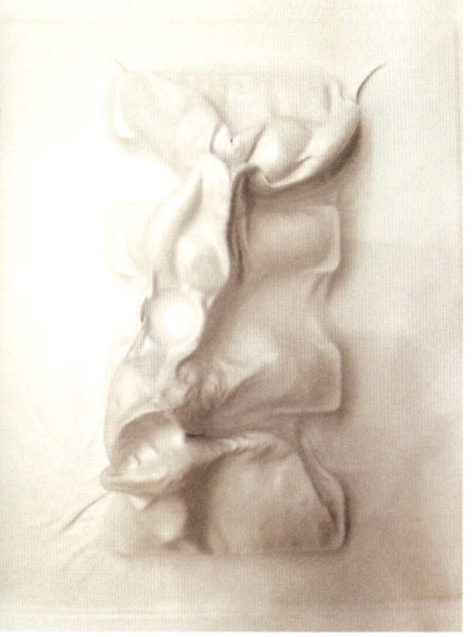

2

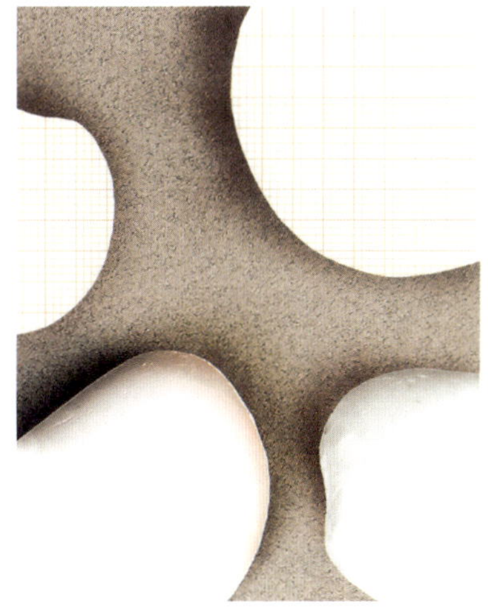

3

4

1 Object collection

2 Vacuum form

3 2-D collage

4 Vacuum form

5

6

7

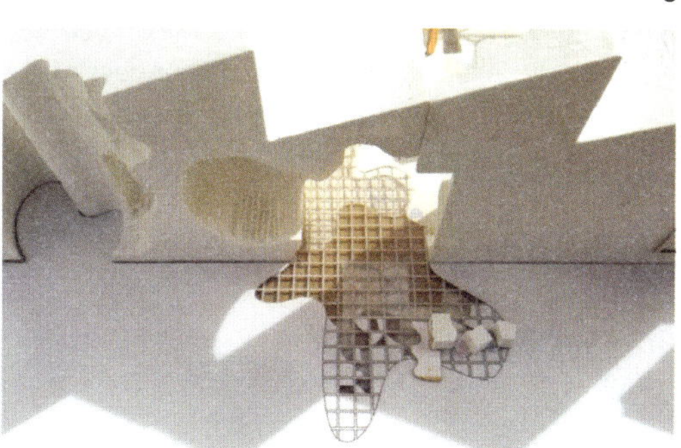

8

5 Exploded axonometric view: warehouse corner

6 Analytic drawing of collaged objects

7 Model, detail: eroded perimeter and cluster formation

8 Model, close-up

Claire Haugh
Cohesive Difference

Our studio defines "easy" work as that which is in fact difficult, complex, excessive, transitional, and implied. Today architecture professionals struggle to produce "easy" work and new aesthetic conditions primarily because it is no longer radical to defamiliarize, copy, and reappropriate in the design process. While it is relatively easy to produce new architectural forms, complex geometries, and provocative representations, it is difficult to realize visual immediacy and complexity that allows for unexpected readings and interpretations.

This project explored the relationship between technology and habitation through "cohesive difference" using familiar and unfamiliar objects. While technological innovations proliferate at an increasing rate, the creative office space remains tied to a stagnant spatial language that, albeit more recently disguised, perpetuates marriage to one's work. The design of office architecture is influenced by advancements in technology, and today automation moves us toward office landscapes where order and uniformity could rule supreme. Systems connect in networks that are inextricably linked and cannot be disconnected. Where does the human fit into this landscape?

The initial collections made for this project explored the deconstruction of highly connected technological objects, such as a computer screen, while new constructions were made from unrelated objects as part of a search for formal ideas that respond to these overlaps and juxtapositions. Expanding this work through collage and a series of drawings allowed me to extract lines, points, and figures to create a series of developed-surface drawings that attempt to generate a "unification of the one interior," as Robin Evans discusses in "The Developed Surface."

The method of relief as a way to generate form derived from a variety of layered elements as the jumping-off point for the project's architectural resolution. The frame became a significant way of referencing both our interaction with technology and a void circulating through space within the "Easy Office" landscape. One can navigate the new formal typologies of furniture, floor, wall, desk, and ceiling/canopy along with framed walkways. The building becomes a way to both occupy a drawing and present new possibilities for offices.

1

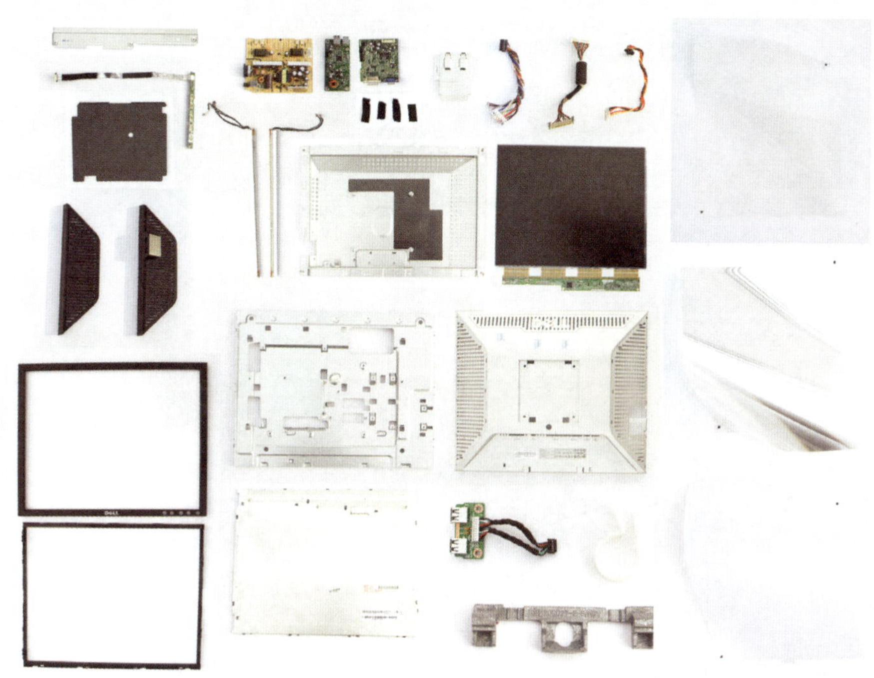

2

3

1 Vacuum form: “Cohesiveness of Difference”

2 Object collection

3 2-D collage

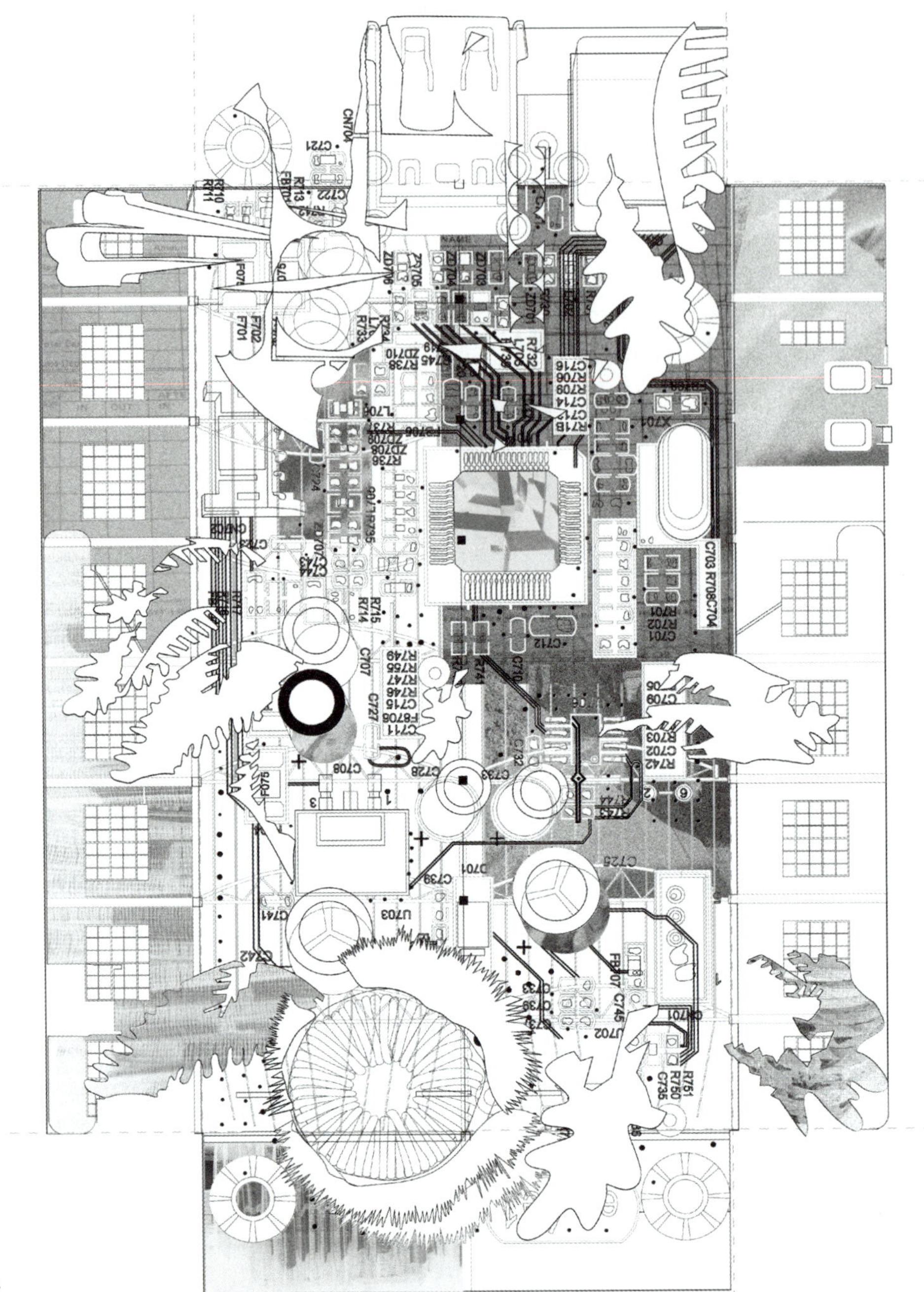

4

4 Developed-surface drawing

5 Screen-print layered drawing

6 Mass and line drawing

7 Laser-cut relief drawing

8 Model as developed-surface drawing

9 Model: "Cohesiveness of Difference" (overleaf)

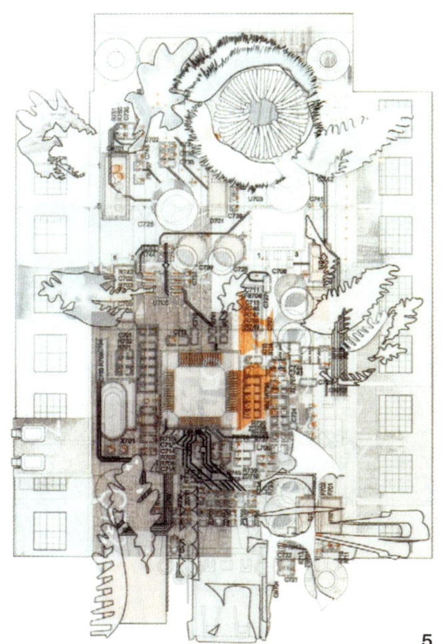

5

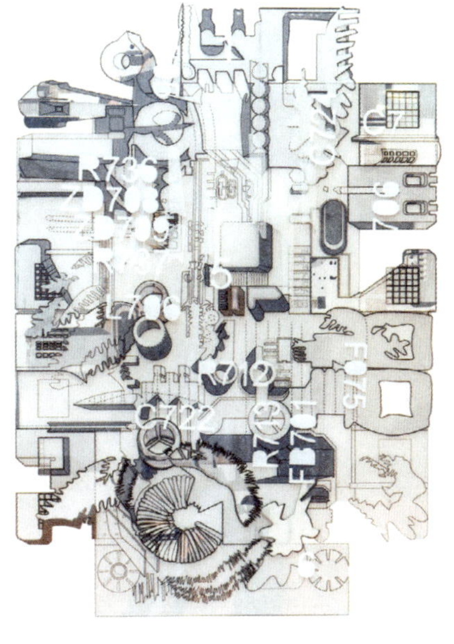

6

7

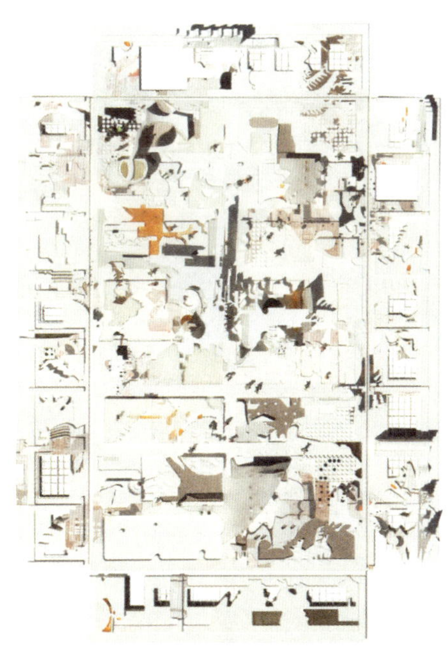

8

9

Andrew Busmire
Incognizant Occupation

"Incognizant Occupation" is a creative office space in Culver City. At the beginning of the studio a series of exercises consolidated qualities of the office typology. A study of readymade objects comprised three operations—collect, collage, and compress—that produced the signature features of the office.

"Incognizant Occupation" challenges the privacy of the current tech office by grafting a private VFX studio and a public work-share space. The first floor is an entirely open-air space accessible from either end of the warehouse, allowing an open floor plan for the work-share space. The interior walls deviate from the exterior shell to create a liner housing circulation for the VFX studio. A thick roof shelters the primary studio space, while "Rooms" house a task-oriented program and project into the work-share space. These rooms carve the ground plane, allowing an interconnected infrastructural system to exist underground. The rooms confront the user of the work-share space, enabling an acknowledgment of a contingent program as well as their own incognizant occupation of the stack.

1

2

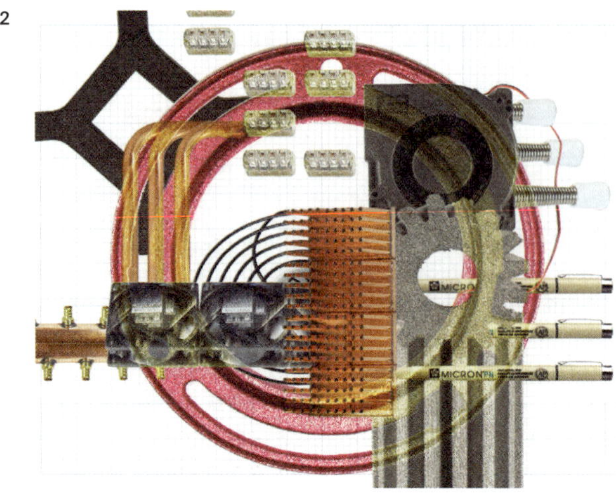

3

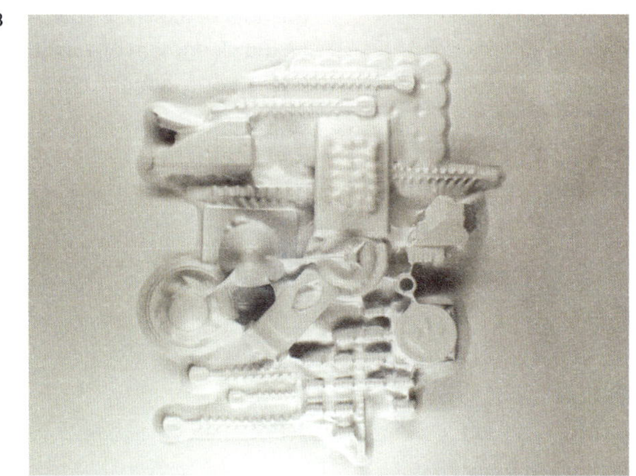

4

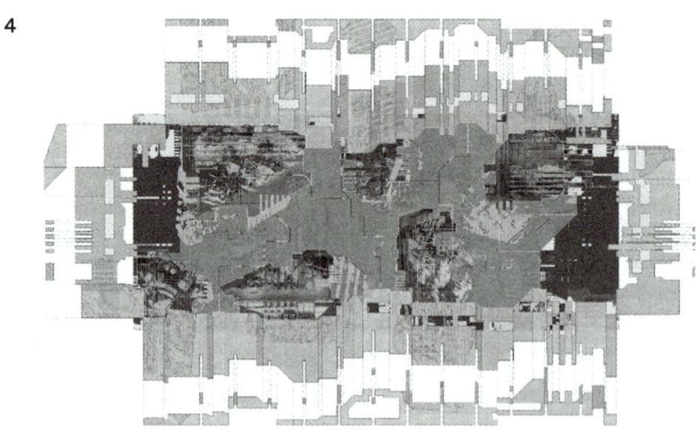

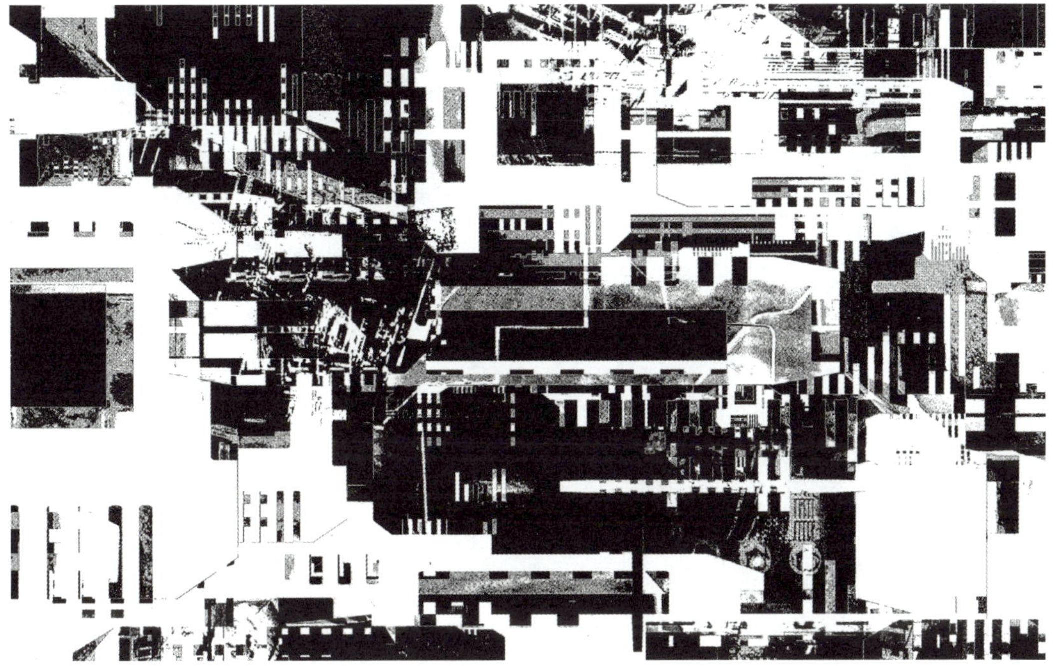

5

6

1 Object collection (previous spread)

2 2-D collage synched

3 Vacuum form

4 Developed-surface grafted medium drawing

5 Contingent overlay

6 Model, detail from ground level

7

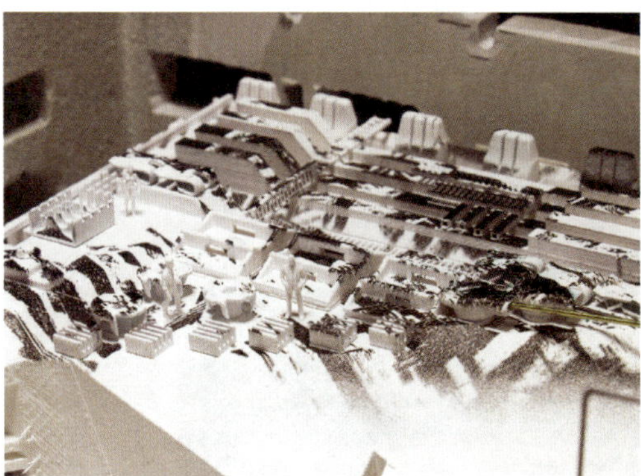

8

7 Model, detail massing

8 Model, detail life

Denisa Buzatu
There's no place like work

The studio looked critically at the work of artists Andy Warhol and Rachel Whiteread as a way to redefine the concept of "easy" work and what it means in the context of today's social, economic, cultural, and aesthetic conditions. Through techniques of collaging, line drawings, and physical model making, the research followed three procedures: collect, compress, and cast.

This project considers a new typology of workplace in which nature is used as a generic element that creates highly specific spaces. Designed with a variety of interchangeable units for both work and living, the office serves remote workers who are linked professionally with Culver City. An ambiguity is achieved in the space through overlapping program layers and activities. Nature acts as the connector between the spaces, constantly shifting between artificial and real.

The building plan takes advantage of its location next to the Ballona Creek and offers a mezzanine pool as a recreational space, while the ground floor mediates between the outdoor and indoor spaces. The side facing the street contains conventional office space with an open floor plan and scattered objects that can be employed as meeting and working spaces. The floor of the building descends to create a visual connection to the creek. The glass pool forms part of the roof, filtering light and creating the sensation of being in an aquarium. A partly open greenhouse located between the conventional street zone and the fluid, more relaxed areas connects the spaces and activities.

1

2

3

4

1 Object collection (previous spread)

2 Preliminary axonometric drawing of building portion

3 2-D collage: studying planes and texture overlapping

4 Vacuum form: nature turns into plastic

5 Developed-surface drawing

5

6

7

6 Top view

7 View from below the swimming pool

8 Greenhouse view

9 Patterns and partitions as space dividers

8

9

Zach Hoffmann
Wallscape

Finding its roots in Andy Warhol's *Brillo Box*, this project engages contemporary work spaces in terms of the "easy" through layered processes of hoarding, collaging, and forming. Office spaces have a history of evolution with various degrees of hierarchies and organizations. Some of the most creative offices today focus on activity-based working and accommodate every type of work situation. This office space seeks to expand on the next generation of creative work spaces through studies of wall typologies, historically a key element in work-space organization due to varying needs for enclosure, acoustic modulation, transparency, and comfort. This project employs an existing warehouse as the shell of the office wallscape.

In the early stages of the project we had to find objects with specific qualities and refine them in a curated hoarding exercise. This collection focused on the cohesion of soft and pudgy, linear and mechanical, and semitransparent variance. The work space assimilates the qualities of the readymades by layering smooth, crusty, and soft surfaces into a single wallscape with varying degrees of enclosure and intimacy. Homogenizing the materiality heightens the textural qualities of the surfaces and blurs their formal origins.

Organized principally through its diagonal orientation, the space breaks the strict rigidity of the existing warehouse grid and produces an immediate sense of disjunction in and identity for the workplace. The configuration allows for visual and formal overlap, in which walls become floors and floors become volumes. A central pathway permeates the diagonal office space and diverges into multiple crossing axes that act as figural gradients. Two exterior spaces bookend the path and fade into a crusty ground.

1

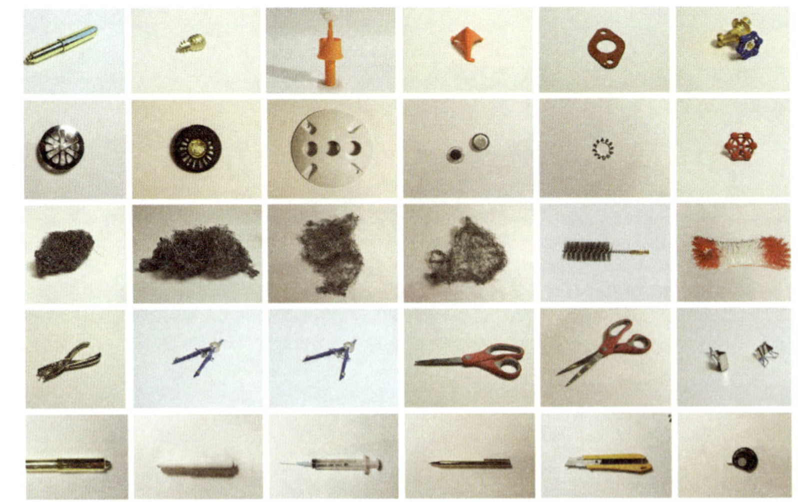

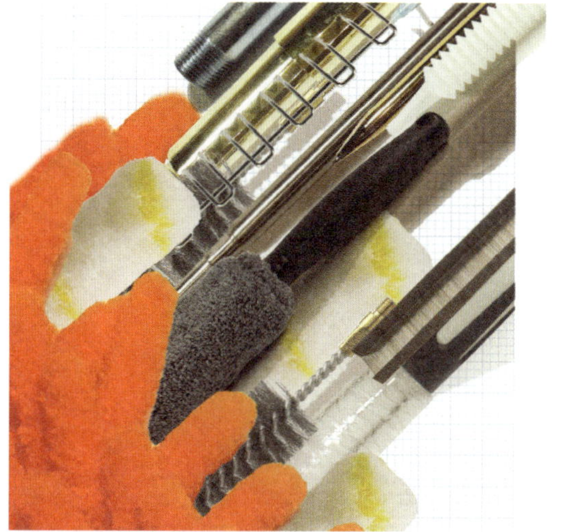

2

3

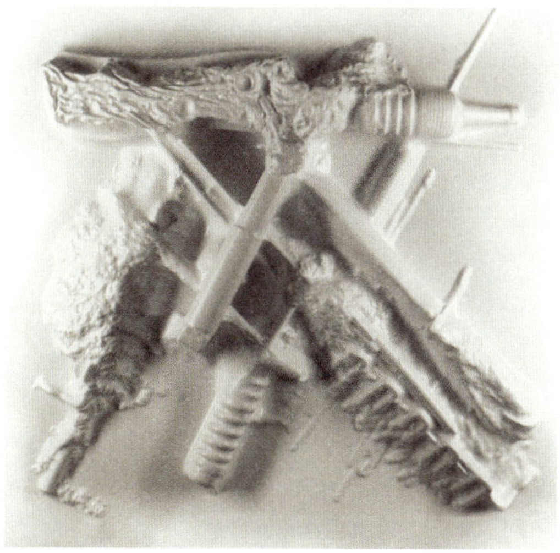

4

5

6

7

(previous spread)

1 Object collection

2 2-D collage, gradient: sleek and pudgy

3 2-D collage: crusty concealment

4 Vacuum form: homogenizing textures

5 Drawing: flattening qualities

6 Model, wallscape

7 Model: work or play?

8

9

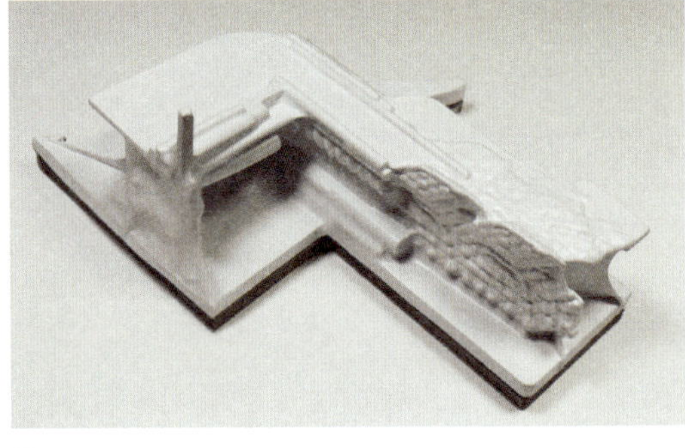

10

8 Model, figural gradients

9 Model, gradated corridors

10 Model, wall chunk

Alex Karlsson-Napp

Shattered Groceries

This office proposal questions the idea of stylistic unity and whether such a thing could be accomplished with diverse parts through a focus on composition and staging rather than brand or thematic straightjackets, resulting in an overarching formality that is inclusive but not oppressive.

When Robin Evans describes the shift from hierarchical space to heterogeneous homogeneity in eighteenth-century English interiors, he notes an unnerving stylistic unity in the setup of domestic scenes, manifesting a "homogenization of appearances" between body, attire, furniture, and architecture. As furniture moves away from the edges or the center, varied elements are "distributed picturesquely across the floor without evident formality," creating a subdivided room of complex and diverse geography. The result is a series of spheres made small and complete enough to function as intimate wholes in a space where nothing departs from an overarching theme.

This proposal for a hypothetical office in Culver City seeks to produce a montage of distinct parts, first combined into a whole and then cut up from that artificial completeness. The parts are shifted to create a series of incomplete wholes in tension with one another. The intent is to make worlds that resist being spherical—that is, closed and hermetic—yet are incomplete and dependent on one another. The forms are bounded and seemingly able to close while leaking and opening up onto one another.

Initially objects were chosen for their aesthetic properties without adherence to any particular theme: fruits as bound volumes with specific colors and textures, translucent objects that allowed for dissolution of these colors and textures, semirigid sheets lacking rigid boundaries able to mold to existing conditions, and duplicate particles allowing for informal conditions. This selection led to a process of designing with densities. In the resulting office space, furniture, and "appearances" are allowed to impact neighboring spaces, resulting in a medley of in-between spaces that "tend toward" rather than "are" something. Pattern and color are seen as methods of defining spaces, as qualities that are adaptable and can gradate rather than form definite boundaries like walls or lines.

1

2

3

1 Collage (previous spread)

2 Drawing process

3 Vacuum form

4 Developed-surface drawing

5

6

5–8 Model, close-up details

7

Margaret Marsh
Organized Chaos

This project demonstrates a space of organized chaos through collecting, collage, drawing, vacuum forming, casting, and axonometric drawing. It is everything at once—a kind of curated hoarding that reflects the wide range of options packed into contemporary creative offices. Through the prioritization of "easy" means and methods, a cacophony of textures, colors, and geometries combine to create an environment layered with imprints of past, present, and future.

In the creative office, equipment is not limited to pairs of desks and chairs. There are lounges, stretching spaces, cafeterias, bars, and so on. Furthermore, these various arrangements of equipment incite loud spaces, quiet spaces, and every sound environment in between. This variety is essential so that work environments can be mixed and matched with unprecedented personalization. It is this breadth of options that this project attempts to explore.

Techniques and strategies are layered and compressed to render an interior space that is both comprehensive and disorienting, a place containing so much information and optionality that it is difficult to navigate. The space folds in office qualities and the site to create a dialogue about the office as a marketplace. Readymade objects are deconstructed and rearranged in an alternative landscape. Clear, pearl, iridescent, and gray resins are layered with paper and styrene to code circulation, programming, and furniture changes. A collection of site photographs determines a field of textures, objects, and sensibilities that relate to both the office space and Culver City. Line and surface blend together through the process of vacuum forming. Real and graphic shadows blur together. Ground materials become physical columns. Patterns extend beyond boundaries. And the office as we know it begins to morph into the image the worker chooses to create.

1

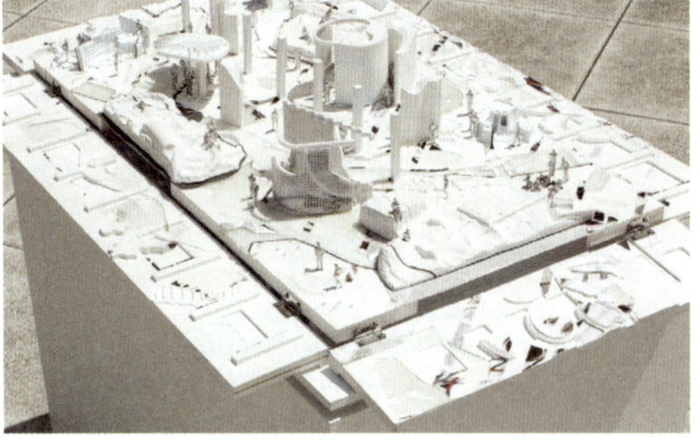

2

1 Model, walls extended down to mirror developed-surface drawing

2 Model, roof framework

3 Shadows and changes in light lending new depth and readings to interior landscape

3

4

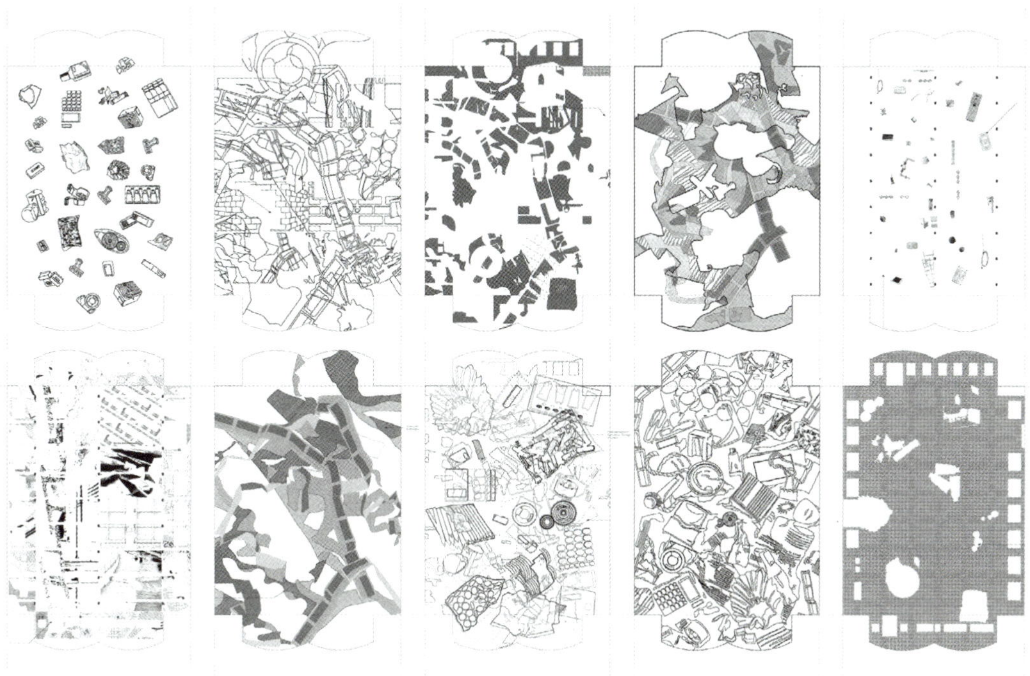

5

6

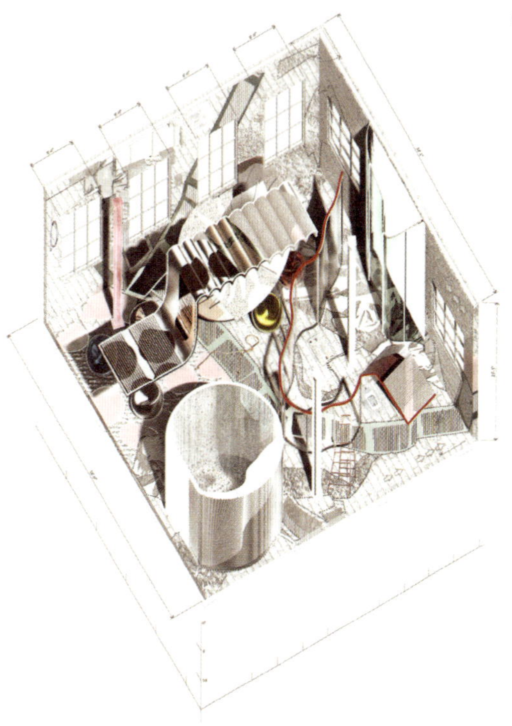

4 Developed-surface drawing

5 Delaminated surface drawings

6 Axonometric drawing, corner portion of project site

7

8

9

7 Collage drawing

8 Cast extracted from vacuum-formed mold

9 Color, tone, and texture palette

Dhruvin Shah
The Office as a Ruin

The initial phase of the studio process hoarded objects ordered into a collection of wooden puzzles displaying characteristics of interlocking, joinery, aggregation, and assembly. Another set was composed of organizing trays, holders, and grills acting as armatures—objects that can self-organize with an almost independent grid system.

The collages and vacuum-formed assemblies highlight the inherent characteristics of the collected objects through aggregation, where there is a breakdown of order due to the multiplicity of armatures within their own independent systems. The extensions using tape created an overlay across objects—revealing aspects of addition, subtraction, and tearing within the order of the objects—and at times exaggerated their qualities. As the objects interwove they either revealed or concealed one another's various parts.

The tectonics reveal a sense of evolution over time as the casts expose an overlay of information and allow the building's existing structure to morph into a new form. The flexible and changing program—such as a coworking spaces, houses, and offices—reflects changing needs. The various operatives evident in the armatures create a fluid and blurred perimeter around the site, in turn producing ambiguity between private and public spaces. The landscape weaves in and out of the periphery, forming covered outdoor spaces. The architectural language indicates form that adapts and overlays its tectonics over time, giving the impression of a public ruin as an open infrastructure of coworking space.

1

1 Collage showing aggregation and overlapping of multiple armatures

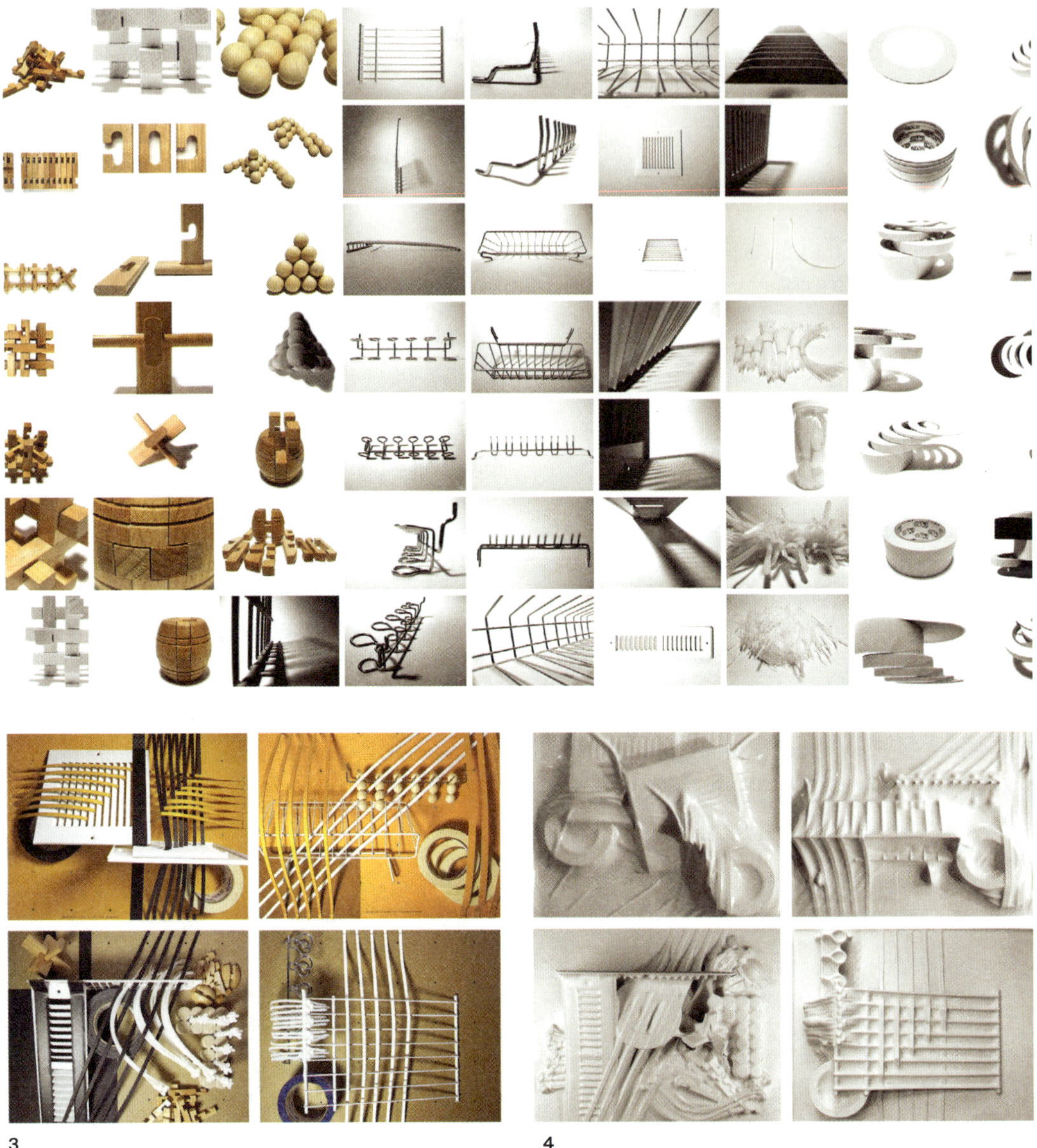

2 Object catalog displaying an inherent order, logics of assembly and aggregation, and a sense of interlocking joinery

3 Physical assemblies locating and clarifying a system of order

4 Object assemblies flattened into a singular topography

5 Developed-surface drawing

6 Notational drawing highlighting aggregation, delineation, and a multiplicity of systems

5

6

7

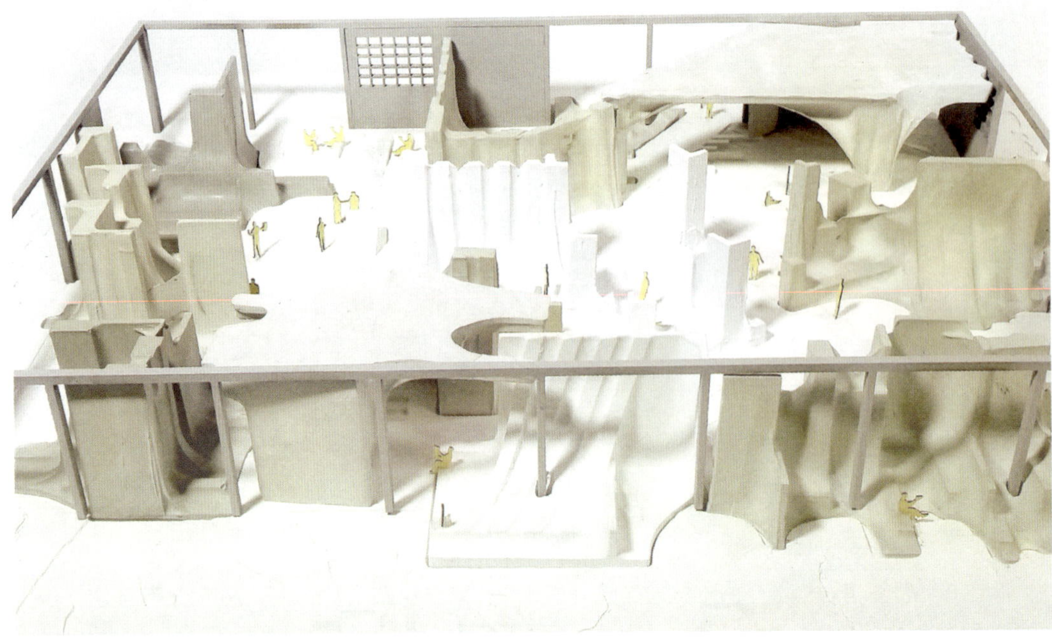

8

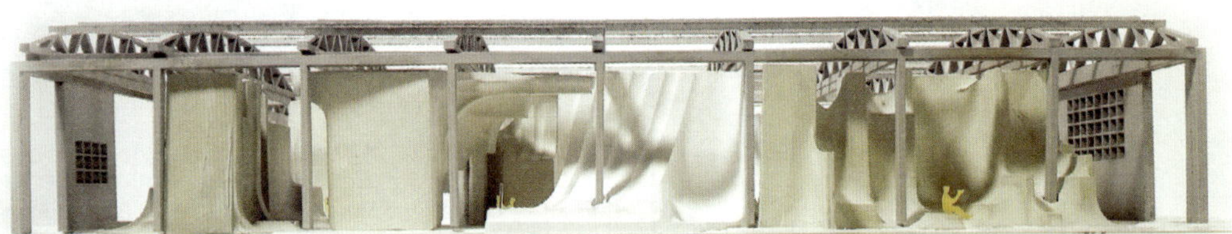

7 Model, overview without roof

8 Model, elevation views

Phineas Taylor-Webb
Soffit Office

Creative office has become a buzzword in contemporary office design with little definition of what the concept implies in terms of space. The rise of mobile digital infrastructure calls into question the purpose of office space altogether. If office space is no longer a necessity, what role will the office have in the future?

While mobile digital infrastructure may have nearly removed the need for traditional offices and amenities, it has not erased the social benefits of collaborative work. Tech offices focus on promoting as much interaction between employees as possible. These social interactions fuel rapid-fire innovation, generating an incredible growth rate. How can the calibration of office space create a range of different social spaces that spark collaboration?

This project demonstrates an interaction between ceiling surface and ground topology. The building's ceiling is derived from processes developed early in the studio. It constitutes a deepened poché allowing for vertical expansion and compression, producing moments of tension and release. The ground topology creates various spaces of social hierarchy calibrated to different uses. The building responds to the lack of green spaces in Hayden Tract by retreating inward from its existing shell. The office enclosure is minimized, and a series of smaller nook gardens are created around the building's perimeter. This verdant buffer creates relief from the stress of work and the pace of the city.

1

2

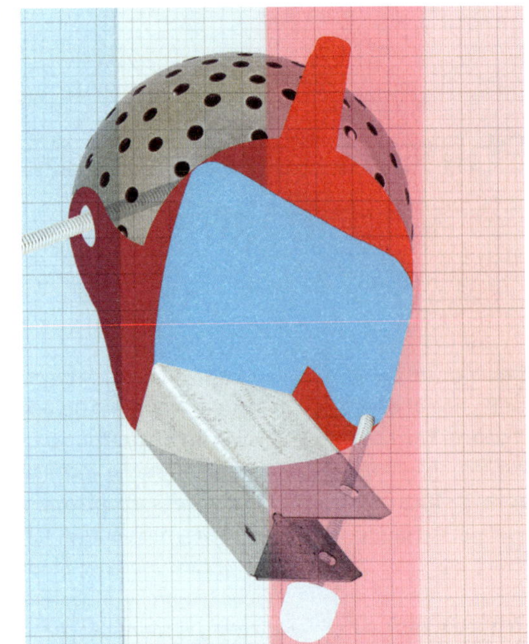

3

4

5

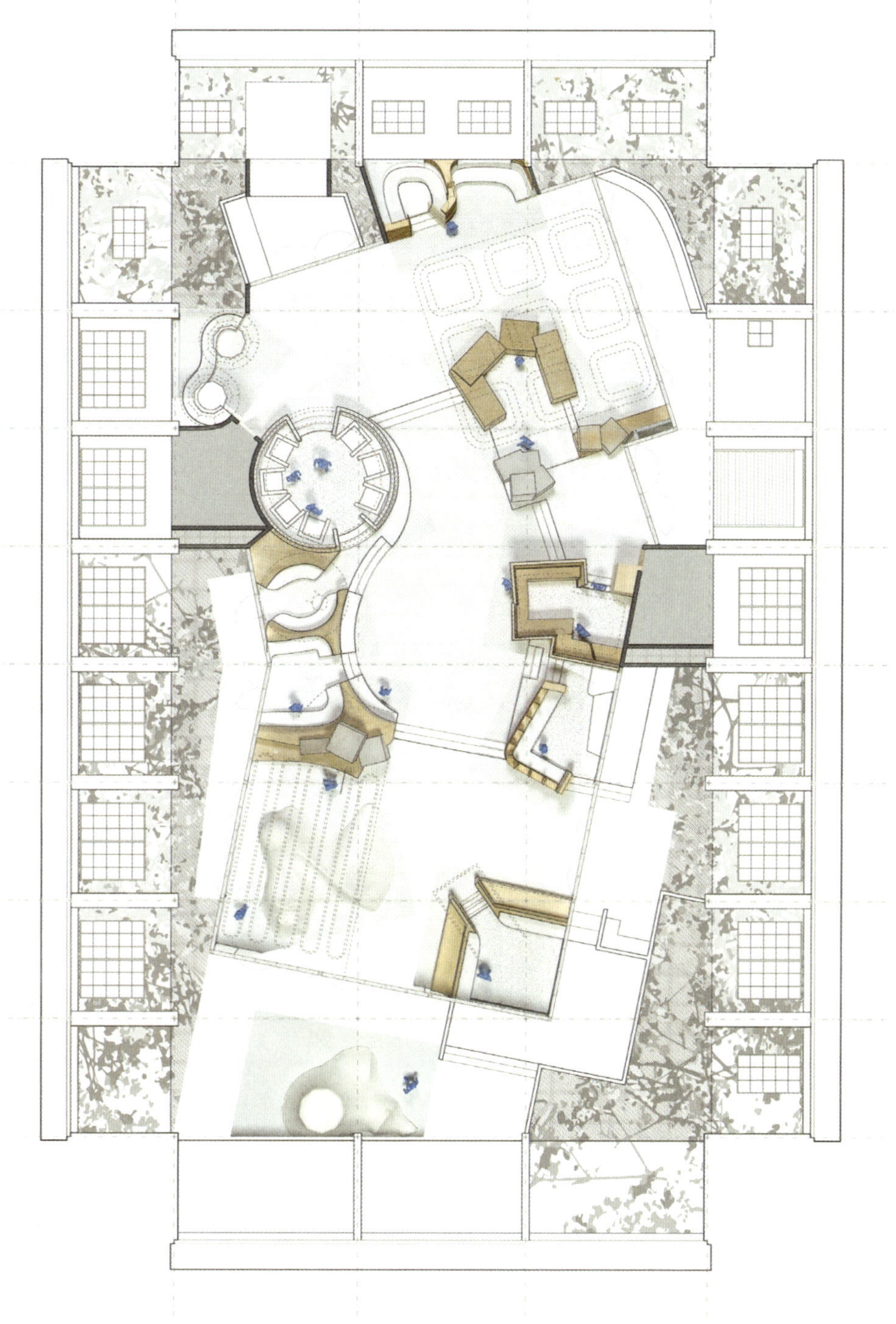

1 Object collection (previous spread)

2 2-D collage

3 3-D collage

4 Vacuum form

5 Developed-surface drawing

6

7

8

6 Interior

7 Reflected ceiling

8 Overview

9 Garden

10 Garden and roof

9

10

Minquan Wang
Differentiated Cohesion

The initial iterations of collection, collage, and compression focused on how objects with highly specific forms can play into a new aggregation that both preserves and contends their individuality. By stitching, deconstructing, approximating, and overlaying, the collaged forms hover between distinct recognizable components and a cohesive whole. The dialectics between difference and cohesion eventually led to a proposal for a next-generation conceptual art studio in the computer-graphics field. Conceptual design bridges art and production, which includes drawing, painting, sculpture, storyboarding, digital painting, 3-D modeling, EFX, and so on. It is a collective endeavor. Artists from various fields negotiate their identities into work in the same "mental space" so that coherent narratives can be produced and communicated to the directors.

The industry is fast paced with an extremely high turnover rate. Conceptual artists traditionally seek employment through a monolithic agency (coherent but slow) or freelance via remote work (efficient but loose). As film and game industries upgrade, they ask for larger-scale collaboration with higher efficiency and more flexibility. This points toward a workplace that allows both specificity in space and synchronization of action. The formal iterations in this studio were transposed into a spatial scheme comprised of two elements: 1) Figures: Forms taken from the collection and site are defamiliarized into individual working spheres. Each one has clearly defined geometry that imposes an organizational order, way of working, or lifestyle. They manifest themselves in enclosures (positive forms), cavities (negative forms), and other space-defining items (walls, ceilings, fixed furniture). 2) Surfaces: Shapes are flattened approximations of the figures reapplied to forms as ambiguous fields devoid of specific formal or programmatic implications. Surfaces are nonautonomous and reliant on the figures to take shape. They either carry a figure to extend its identity or cover a figure to obscure it yet take its shape simultaneously.

The play between the figures and surfaces results in a versatile workscape that shifts between identifiable forms and fluid aggregations. Conceptual artists find their temporary niches and constantly shuffle as projects proceed. They mingle and transform as the layers of spaces overlap and negotiate. The workplace is neither fixed nor amorphous.

1

2

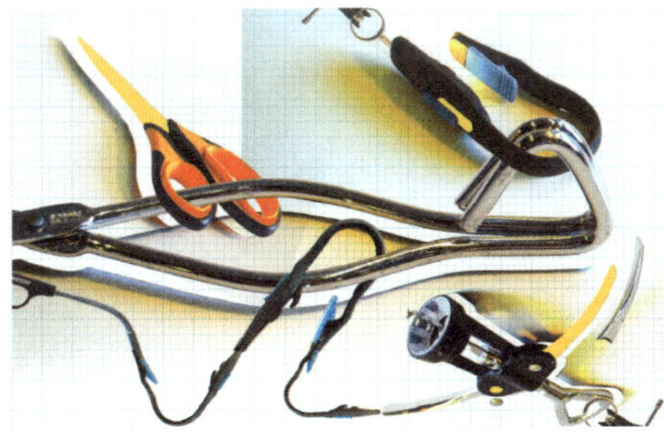

3

1 Object collection

2 A Frankenstein of daily items

3 Monochrome vacuum form of 3-D collage

4

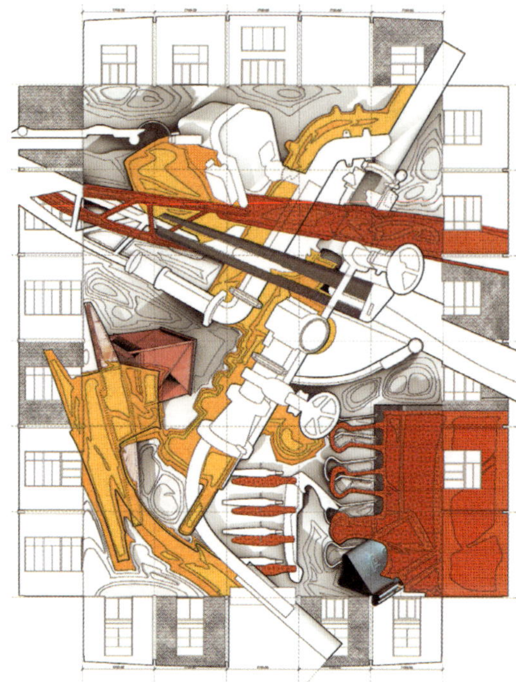

5

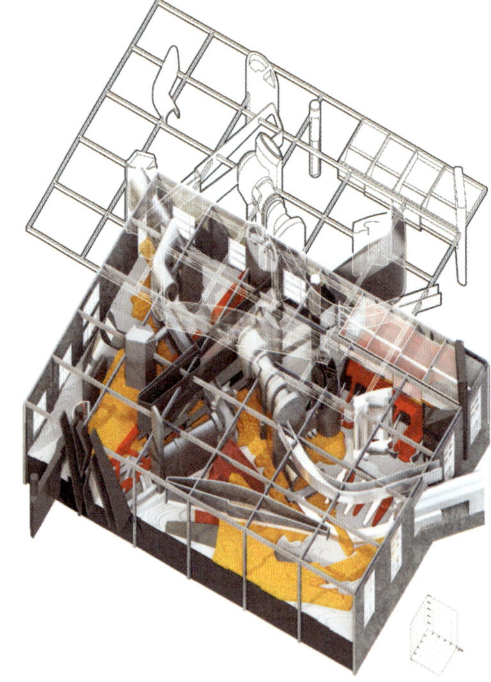

6

4 Developed-surface drawing

5 Axonometric drawing with isolated ceiling

6 Model, top view with ceiling

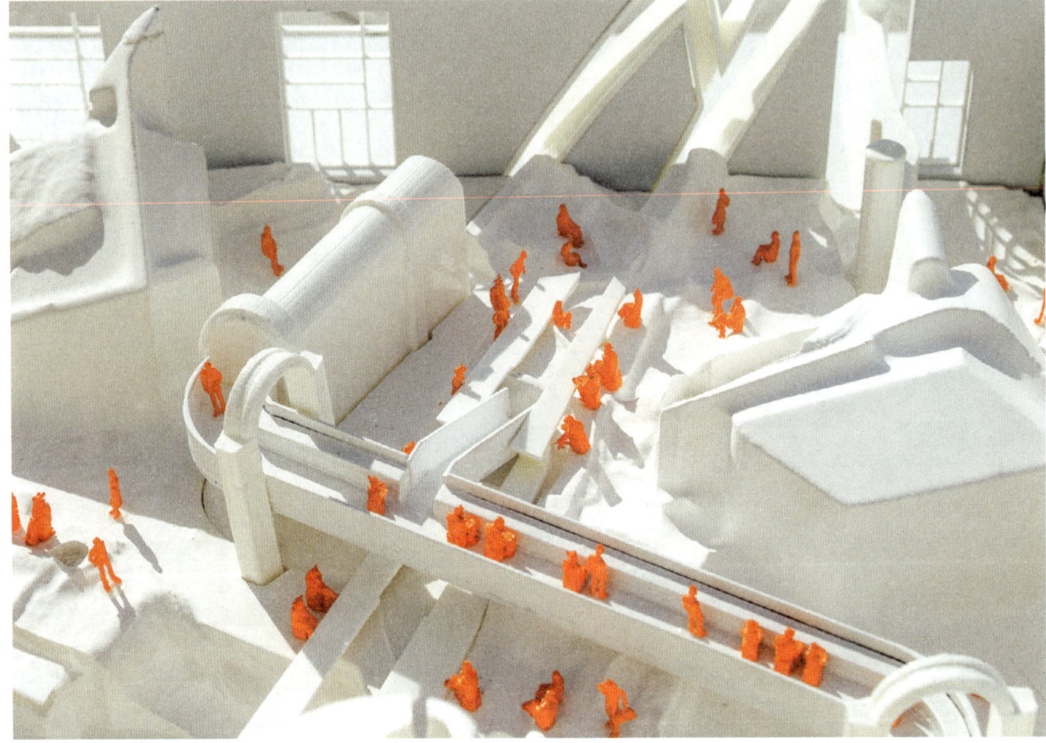

7

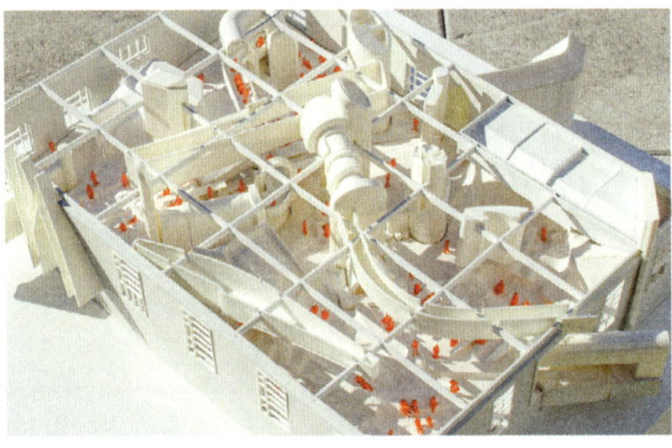

8

9

7 Model, figures reconstructed via developed-surface method

8 Model, overview

9 Model, ceiling meeting floor

Image Credits

Florencia Pita and Jackilin Hah Bloom: 5, 7, 8

Andy Warhol (1928-1987) © Copyright, Davis Museum at Wellesley College / Art Resource, NY: 12

Lisane Skyler. *Brillo Box (3¢ Off)*, documentary, HBO, 2016: 13

Rachel Whiteread. *Untitled (Twenty-Five Spaces)*, National Gallery of Art, photograph by Nina Rappaport: 14

Sharmin Bhagwagar: 26, 27, 28, 29

Claire Haugh: 30, 31, 32, 33, 34

Andrew Busmire: 35, 36, 37, 38

Denisa Buzatu: 39, 40, 41, 42, 43

Zach Hoffman: 44, 45, 46, 47, 48

Alex Karlsson-Napp: 49, 50, 51, 52, 53

Margaret Marsh: 54, 55, 56, 57, 58

Dhruvin Shah: 59, 60, 61, 62

Phineas Taylor-Webb: 63, 64, 65, 66, 67

Minquan Wang: 69, 70, 71, 72

Omar Gandhi

Contents

Conversation between Nina Rappaport and Omar Gandhi

NINA RAPPAPORT: As a Canadian architect you are known for your local inspirations. How does the intensity of the natural environment, especially the extremes of weather and terrain, influence you?

OMAR GANDHI: As architects we are always looking for constraints, and here we are spoiled with them because things are so dramatic. In Nova Scotia we are confronted with really wild landscapes so that each project, whether on a tall, rocky cliff line or an inland field, varies quite a bit. Climate and context inform the first moves we make.

NR: What intrigues you about basic architectural forms such as the "primitive hut"? How do you translate vernacular traditions into the contemporary without making them cliché?

OG: Aside from the obvious beauty, architecture draws on nostalgia, on memories of childhood. I wouldn't know where to start if not for truths about where materials come from and why the roof is shaped just so. Architecture has been influenced by a series of experiments over a long period of time, drawing on the way it acutely responds to materials and climate and landscape. We have a lot of fun with it, whether it's the way a roof shelters the facade like a cap does your brow or how to protect a doorway. I remember at one of my first jobs I drew a Modernist long building in northern Ontario. My boss took his pencil and drew a big mound on the roof and asked, "Do you know what that is? It's ten feet of snow on the roof. It doesn't make sense then, does it?" That has always stuck in my mind.

NR: Why did you study architecture, and what have been some of the best moments of your education in Canada?

OG: In my family, as well as my culture, the arts aren't an avenue that is encouraged, even though the latest Pritzker Prize winner is from India, as is my family. What's encouraged is sciences and engineering. My father is a microbiologist with a passion for the arts, and he encouraged me to go down that road. I went to an arts high school and University of Toronto to study art history and visual arts. I was attracted to architecture as a path, and I found peace and enjoyment in that process as well. I was very lucky to go to Dalhousie University School of Architecture and Planning, in Halifax. The school was kind of behind the times in terms of technology and it emphasized making things by hand, whether wood models or actual buildings. I didn't have a lot of technical knowledge, so going out in the field to make things was special.

NR: Craft plays a huge role in your projects, including the use of local materials and craftspeople. How did you engage with contractors such as Deborah Herman-Spartinelli, and how did you start in this direction with such care?

OG: The craft tradition is rich in this part of the world, and it comes from a culture of pride. The main thing is that our work is not very expensive. We don't have quartz backsplashes and copper roofs in Nova Scotia, which is very different from Ontario, where people spend an enormous amount of money. The beauty comes from the care in the work. Part of finding workers is to understand what they've done previously, but it's really just about sitting down and talking to them about what their own ambitions are. We don't work with large builders that churn things out; we're working with people who want to make a name and work on our projects because they're excited to be part of something special.

NR: Do you work directly with contractors on-site?

OG: I used to do that, and now I go maybe once every other time. I miss that aspect. Jeff Shaw, who's been my associate from almost the beginning, and Stephanie Hosein, in Toronto, work closely with the builders in an

Omar Gandhi Architect, Rabbit Snare Gorge, Inverness, Nova Scotia, 2016

ongoing dialogue. We convince clients that the CA phase of a project, when things are actually being built, is the most important because that's where we form trust and dialogue with the builder toward the end result. Deborah was the first builder I worked with on my own, and she became a mentor. If not for her, I certainly would not have gotten the second job.

NR: Does your Indian heritage influence your architecture?

OG: I've only been to India once. My family came to Canada in the 1950s; my parents were raised in Canada or England. My mom grew up in Montreal and worked at "Man and His World," the legacy exposition at the site of Expo 67. Our family was very social—there were always tons of people coming over—and I see the difference from our clients' family lives. Because we were different it forces me to pay attention to the uniqueness of family relationships and the way families interact. When I was a kid, before people started making more money in Canada, everyone had small houses; but we were a gigantic family and had lots of family events all the time. My earliest memories are of everybody sitting on the floor in a circle, and that's how we would eat together. I'm kind of sad about that now because although people have bigger houses they aren't necessarily used

Omar Gandhi Architect, Rabbit Snare Gorge, Inverness, Nova Scotia, 2016

Omar Gandhi Architect, Sluice Point, Yarmouth, Nova Scotia, 2017

to sitting cross-legged on the floor, so everyone's sitting at tables. That dynamic has changed so much.

NR: How does this impact your design of houses? Do you become a kind of therapist for the clients?

OG: I think it's important to be acutely aware of the uniqueness of individual families, and that's one of our strengths. Our work is at a high level because we are very emotional people that are invested in these relationships. I often wish I was a bit more detached because it's difficult go to bed at night when you want other people to be happy. It's a constant struggle with the mind. There is no balance.

NR: How is your firm organized now that you have offices in both Halifax and Toronto, and do you work out of both?

OG: The Halifax office started in 2010 in my attic, then I had a small space with one staff member. After eight years we had five people in Halifax, and two years ago we opened up the Toronto office. For the last three years I have been going back and forth every four days. Often we all jump on one project if there is a deadline. We have stayed small so we can be selective

Omar Gandhi Architect, Sluice Point, Yarmouth, Nova Scotia, 2017

about the kinds of projects and clients we take on. It allows us to be a little bit selfish.

NR: How has your approach to context differed from one place to another—for example, from rural areas to Toronto?

OG: I would say that it's exactly the same. It's really about investigating the context, but in the urban case it's just more zoomed in. It is the contextual background of neighborhoods and their inhabitants, the materials and scale, the streetscape and rhythm. Working on a cottage in a field with nothing around it for miles is very different, but the process is exactly the same. Instead of the vernacular agrarian forms in Nova Scotia, we are looking at simple postwar brick homes that follow a certain datum line and roof shape in Toronto. It might lead to results that are less dynamic because of the stricter relationships with existing buildings. In the noise of urban architecture, especially in a city like Toronto, everyone is constantly trying to come up with ideas that are good for resale, and I'm not really interested in that. By being quiet in that context, you're almost making a louder impact.

NR: The Rabbit Snare Gorge cabin was instrumental to your career in terms of its exaggerated proportions, and your new forms are increasingly experimental. What were the design processes for the Syncline and Sluice Point houses, for example?

OG: We spent a lot of time thinking about the general massing, so although Syncline is a very modern house on a fairly traditional street, it's a big lot. The house had different vantage points toward a view right in front of it over a series of houses below. It was about getting up as high as possible and utilizing the maximum outdoor space, but we allowed ourselves to be more free of local constraints than usual. The idea for the Sluice Point project was to be as quiet as possible: when you squint your eyes it looks like an extension of the landscape, likened to haystacks in marshy landscapes. The concept was to be as lean and long as possible through a dynamic form.

NR: What upcoming project are you most excited about?

OG: We're working on two restaurants in Toronto, something we haven't done before. One of them is for chef Matty Matheson, a big star on Viceland TV, and it will be highly crafted to suit both the city and our existing body of work. The intensity of the project seems appropriate for Matheson, a very large man covered in tattoos who basically swears nonstop.

NR: Is it the biological forms or the performance of nature in biomimicry, in terms of integration with the built environment, that you are most interested in here?

OG: I am interested in biomimicry that doesn't necessarily look like nature but is connected to and survives on the land. It is like walking in a field and understanding why certain species of plants are the way they are and where they are located, depending on proximity to the sun or to moist land. It is about architecture at the next level of regionalism. You draw not only from local materials and building methods but also from the immediate resources of the land. Architecture needs water, sunlight, and protection from the wind, just the way plant species do. How does that impact the overall form and the way a building works, in terms of the smallest details and on a formal level? How does this shape our experience and connection to the land as inhabitants? These are the things I'm really interested in and started to explore as part of my research for the Prix de Rome. It's going to be a lifelong study.

This discussion was published in the Fall 2018 issue of *Constructs*.

Omar Gandhi Architect, Syncline House, Halifax, Nova Scotia, 2017

Where the Wild Things Are

The crux of Maurice Sendak's *Where the Wild Things Are* (1963) is that our environment is transformed by imagination, embodied in a solitary child named Max who is liberated from confinement by his visions. The story centers on ideas of growth, survival, and change inspired by real and fictive worlds. What is the impact of envisioning a new landscape and then returning to the world we came from? Where do ephemeral experiences crafted by the mind intersect with the physical world? Imagination is the tool used to construct the framework of experience. Comparing the themes of this story to the practice of biomimicry in architecture may lead to a convergence of ideas that fall somewhere between humankind vs. nature and humankind vs. imagined nature.

Architecture is essentially an art form of reconciliation and mediation, and in addition to settling us in space and place, landscapes and buildings articulate our experiences of duration and time between the polarities of past and

> future. ... Memory and fantasy, recollection and imagination, are related and they have always a situational and specific content. One who cannot remember can hardly imagine because memory is the soil of imagination. Memory is also the ground of self-identity; we are what we remember.
>
> —Juhani Pallasmaa

We must confront and deconstruct the simplistic binary definitions distinguishing natural and constructed environments: art vs. science, imaginary vs. built, phenomenology vs. technology, theory vs. practice. Perhaps these are not dichotomous but related—fundamental even to the perception and understanding of landscape and place. In this Yale studio project the students mediated between past inheritance and future potential to transcend a limited binary way of thinking. The project transitioned from imagined space to actualized place through responsive processes.

Phenomenological opportunities were explored to create a unique architecture of "place" through climatically responsive design. Students explored progressive strategies for diverting, mitigating, and integrating climate—in all its forms—through and within the built environment. We explored the evolution of architectural responses to building in Inverness, Nova Scotia, an area of extreme climatic conditions. Through a blend of traditional and contemporary means, our intent was to evolve a methodology of climatically responsive, regionally inspired architecture.

The landscape of Rabbit Snare Gorge is defined by the steep slopes of the Cape Breton Highlands: dense woodland with patches of Acadian hardwood, deep gorges cut by a babbling brook, and the rocky cliffs of the Northumberland Strait. The location allows for a long, wide view of the entire property including the majority of the gorge leading toward the ocean.

Lawrence MacIsaac recalls stories of his great grandfather using the property to teach his sons how to snare rabbits, while his great grandmother commonly used the "laundry stone" at the bottom of a small waterfall to wash clothing. The steeply sloped sides of the gorge made it difficult to do anything with the land, including logging, so it was left to grow wild.

The cabin at Rabbit Snare Gorge is the first of three small structures resembling creatures hidden in the mysterious landscape. The cabin is the primary dwelling on the land, and its gabled tower reaches above the forest canopy with two major viewing platforms, one oriented directly toward the ocean and the other along the length of the convergent brook valley. The procession through the cabin starts with the entry and bedrooms on the ground floor, a double-height kitchen and dining room on the second floor, and a living space on the third floor, along with the lookout view of the entire property.

The structure is linked to the local vernacular through a number of formal elements. The cabin's traditional gable form is manipulated to open views and follows the path of the sun, emphasizes the main interior spaces, and accentuates the verticality of the tower while efficiently shedding snow and rain. Traditional local wood-board cladding is used on the exterior. The cabin's steel entry hoop takes shape from the entry windbreaks, a form unique to the Cape Breton and Newfoundland coastal communities.

How can a house be light on the land and yet sturdy against the wind? The client is an avid outdoorsman and hobby arborist with a sincere respect for the natural landscape. Therefore sensitivity to site and ecological disruption was an early and major design parameter. The cabin's tower typology offers views and ample programming within a minimal footprint. The exposure of the sloped site means it endures the full brunt of heavy Atlantic rainstorms, winter nor'easters, corrosive salty spray from crashing swells, and strong *suêtes*—local southeasterly winds that accelerate down the highland escarpment to reach speeds of more than 200 kilometers per hour.

The strong winds demand robust structural systems to withstand major lateral loads and uplift. The tall cabin resists the high winds through redundant sheathing—every solid plane, including the interior partition wall, contributes as shear wall, diaphragm, and stacked compression ring. The windbreak, constructed of welded weathering steel, is hung from the framing.

How can future constructions take cues from this tower and find new strategies for resisting the climatic forces of the site? In the search for meaning through the medium of architecture, Omar Gandhi Architect strives to implant our structures deeply into the context. The phenomenological qualities of climate—rain, sleet, and hail, the presence of sunlight and shadow, the turn of the seasons—provide depth to our architectural narrative. The elements that shape the landscape in turn shape our architecture. Placed within the global context of a collective environmental awareness, regional architectural discourse should evolve beyond its role as a barrier against the elements toward a more integrated model in which the functional elements form an essential part of the architecture aesthetics.

Human memory is acquired; we are born with a clean slate upon which experience makes its marks. As with the human, so with the built environment. Most societies respect the aged as sources of a wisdom acquired through time and experience. Buildings and landscapes too can acquire wisdom in their fabrics. They can tell us things, should we choose to ask and listen—and of course, assuming we know their language.

...The structure or landscape may provoke memories, but its construction, use, and modification over time in itself embodies memories then passed on to the next generation of visitors. This process is a give and take between the environment, the individual, and society as a group. Thus, we might say that there are both memories in and memories (projected) upon our built environment. They become repositories into which, and from which, like a bank, both deposits and withdrawals may be transacted: the built environment as a memory bank, both individual and communal.

—Marc Treib, *Spatial Recall: Memory in Architecture and Landscape*

Omar Gandhi Architect, Rabbit Snare Gorge, Inverness, Nova Scotia, 2016

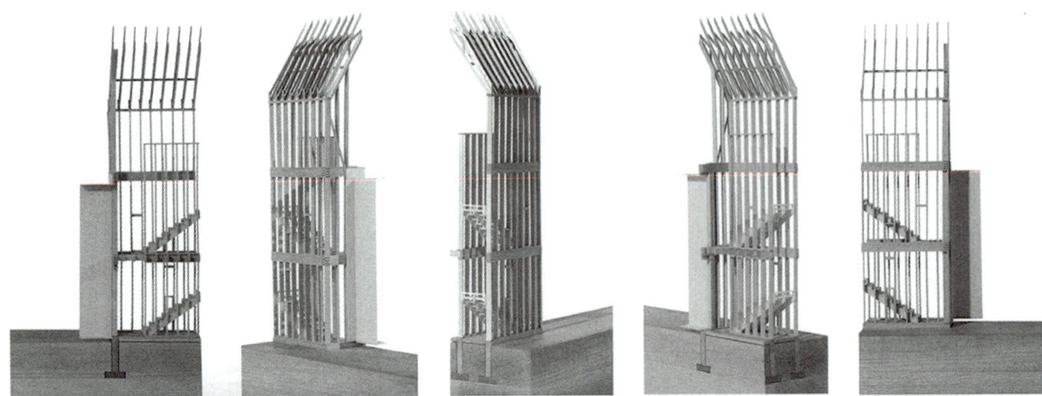

Structural models for Rabbit Snare Gorge

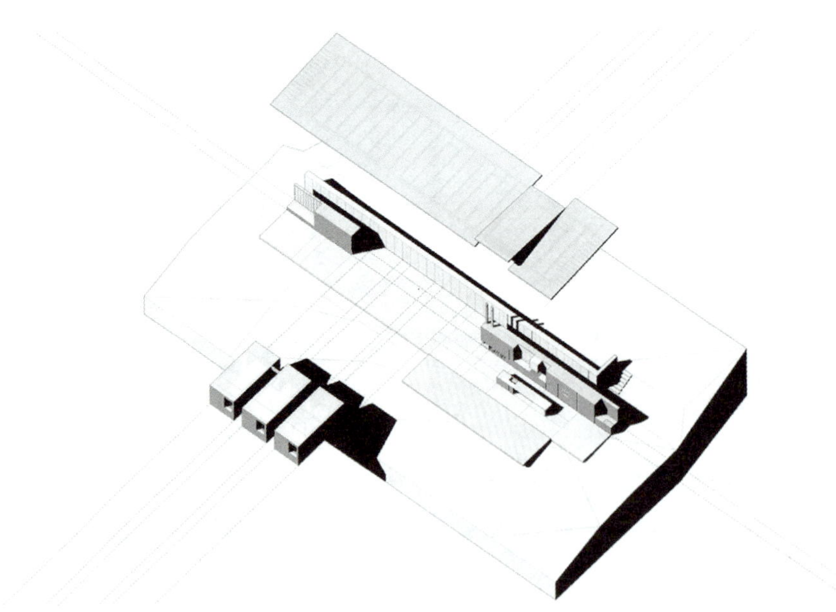

Axonometric drawing of the Lookout at Broad Cove March showing siting and assembly strategies

Omar Gandhi Architect, the Lookout at Broad Cove Marsh, Inverness, Nova Scotia, 2015

Studio Brief

This studio proposed the challenge of designing a "campus of creatures"—a series of interventions that use vernacular approaches to produce specific functional qualities, develop a process or ideology, and frame sensory experience—on the property of Rabbit Snare Gorge. A unique architecture of "place" would take advantage of the phenomenological opportunities available on the site. Students explored progressive strategies for diverting, mitigating, and integrating various manifestations of climate through and within the built environment. They also investigated the evolution of architectural responses to building in a region of extreme climatic conditions, particularly Inverness, Nova Scotia. The students researched climatically responsive, regionally inspired architecture employing a blend of traditional and contemporary approaches.

Site Opportunities

Architectural systems can respond or adapt to, or even mimic, local environmental processes. Students developed an awareness of the naturally constructed relationships in the region to navigate the complexities of both the environmental and built contexts. How do environmental conditions transform throughout the year? And how is local culture and architecture impacted? The studio considered the dimensions of the site and visited important regional buildings, experiencing social rituals and observing how local architecture is produced. The students also took account of conditions such as sunlight, wind, ground, and local vegetation.

Organization

The first project considered the primitive hut as a device to mitigate a specific climatic element: light, wind, or water. Working in teams, students designed an architectural system that responded to one of these environmental conditions at a site of their own selection on Yale's campus. Each project manipulated a large tarp to achieve the basic criteria of shelter and security while reshaping notions of how architectural form may develop through a close relationship to the natural world. Results were recorded in drawings, sketch models, and photographs of the interventions.

The resulting forms were analyzed and developed through physical and digital modeling. The single manipulated plans were translated into more complex envelopes with performance characteristics such as transparency, porosity, and thickness. Students further manipulated and adapted their forms based on a related narrative that introduced a character and her or his requirements. The program or experience underscored a symbiotic relationship between environmental conditions, design elements, and users. Student teams constructed sectional models demonstrating the primary aspects of each scheme as it related to their respective elements; adaptations also took shape through plan and section drawings.

The second project considered the physical, cultural, and climatic conditions of the site in both local and regional contexts. The students conducted a collective site analysis, gathered regional climatic data, and analyzed responsive building methods in the local architectural vernacular. Digital and physical models documented the topography, wind, sun, precipitation, views, trees, historical precedents, local materials and building typologies. Students selected a specific location on the site to place interventions, and throughout the travel week each developed an initial response, program, and/or experience based on systems developed in the first project.

Following travel week and site analysis, the students integrated site and contextual analyses with previously explored methods of climatically responsive design. For midterm they developed a formal implementation of ideas and methodologies in a carefully sited pavilion. The project housed a specific program, facilitated a relationship between the natural and constructed environments, and distilled a connection to different elements in a continually changing environment. In addition to a singular prototype, students prepared an aggregation strategy to organize the site at Rabbit Snare Gorge and a larger campus of interventions.

After midterm each student incorporated their pavilion into a larger "campus of creatures" at Rabbit Snare Gorge, which served as an outdoor camp for children. While the students determined specific programs and activities for campers, the main objectives were for children to experience the great outdoors, learn respect for the natural environment, and gain an understanding of the local landscape. Students focused on how architectural systems respond to climate at multiple scales to generate wonderful experiences for pint-size users throughout all four seasons.

The site at Rabbit Snare Gorge encompasses many geological, topological, and ecological conditions.

Site condition: gorge

Site condition: brook mouth

Site condition: rocky bottom

Site condition: seasonal stream

Site condition: birch grove

Site condition: wildflower meadow

Site condition: natural clearing

Site condition: cascade

Meat Cove, Cape Breton Island, Nova Scotia

The Fortress of Louisbourg, Cape Breton Island, Nova Scotia

Student Work

Benjamin Olsen
The Lodges at Broad Cove Banks

The lodges at Broad Cove Banks shape the ground using the retaining wall as a primary architectural device. Here ground is not a background element against which figures are understood but the primary material for place and space making. The "thickened ground" of Broad Cove Banks hosts space, circulation, and landscaping. Long lines of architecture and landscape are inscribed along the contours, blending into the grade. The buildings lodge into the ground, their narrow width and prolonged length creating volume without apparent mass. The walls slip and splay to organize space, circulation, and landscaping. They define edges and levels, produce gaps for sunlight and entry, and distinguish between enclosed and open space. Lodging the campus in the thickened ground suggests that we don't just tread on this earth but belong to it.

1

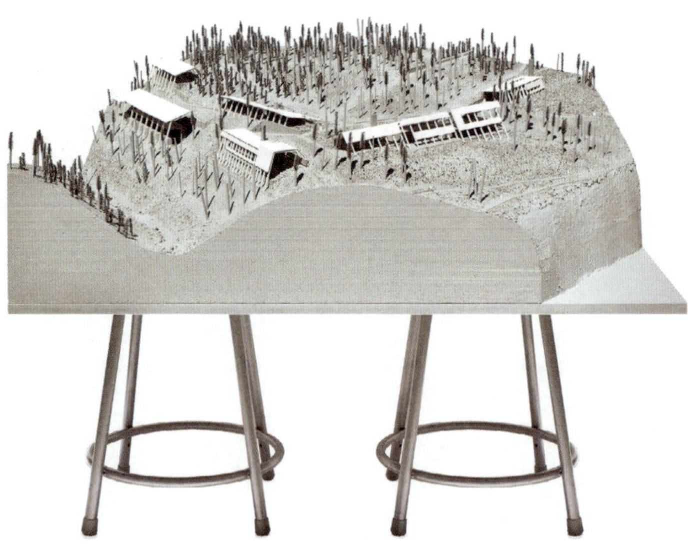

2

1 Schematic model

2 Broad Cove Banks

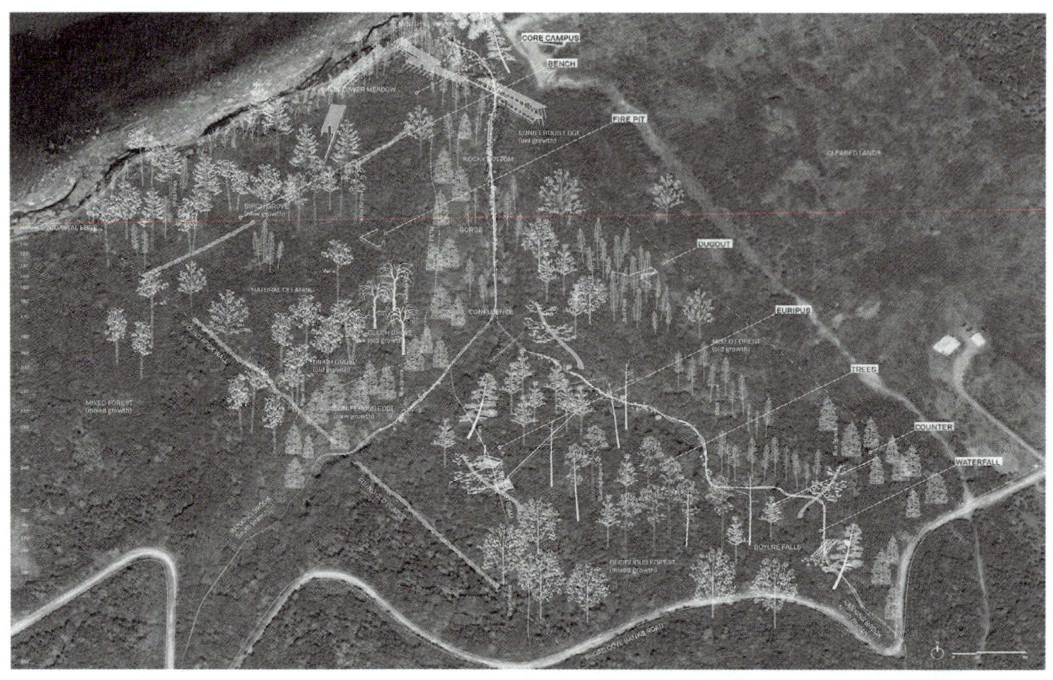

3

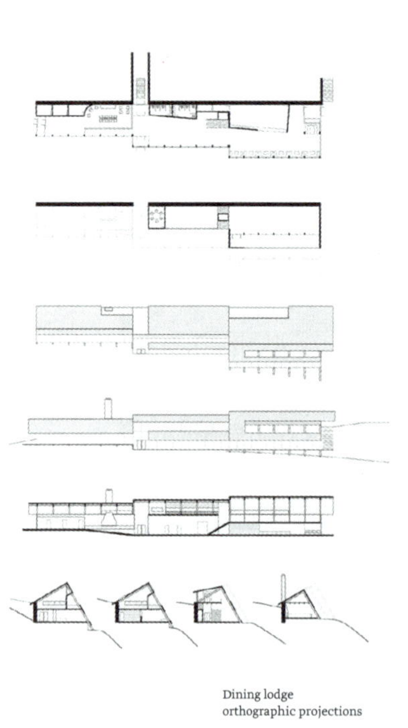

Dining lodge
orthographic projections

4

5

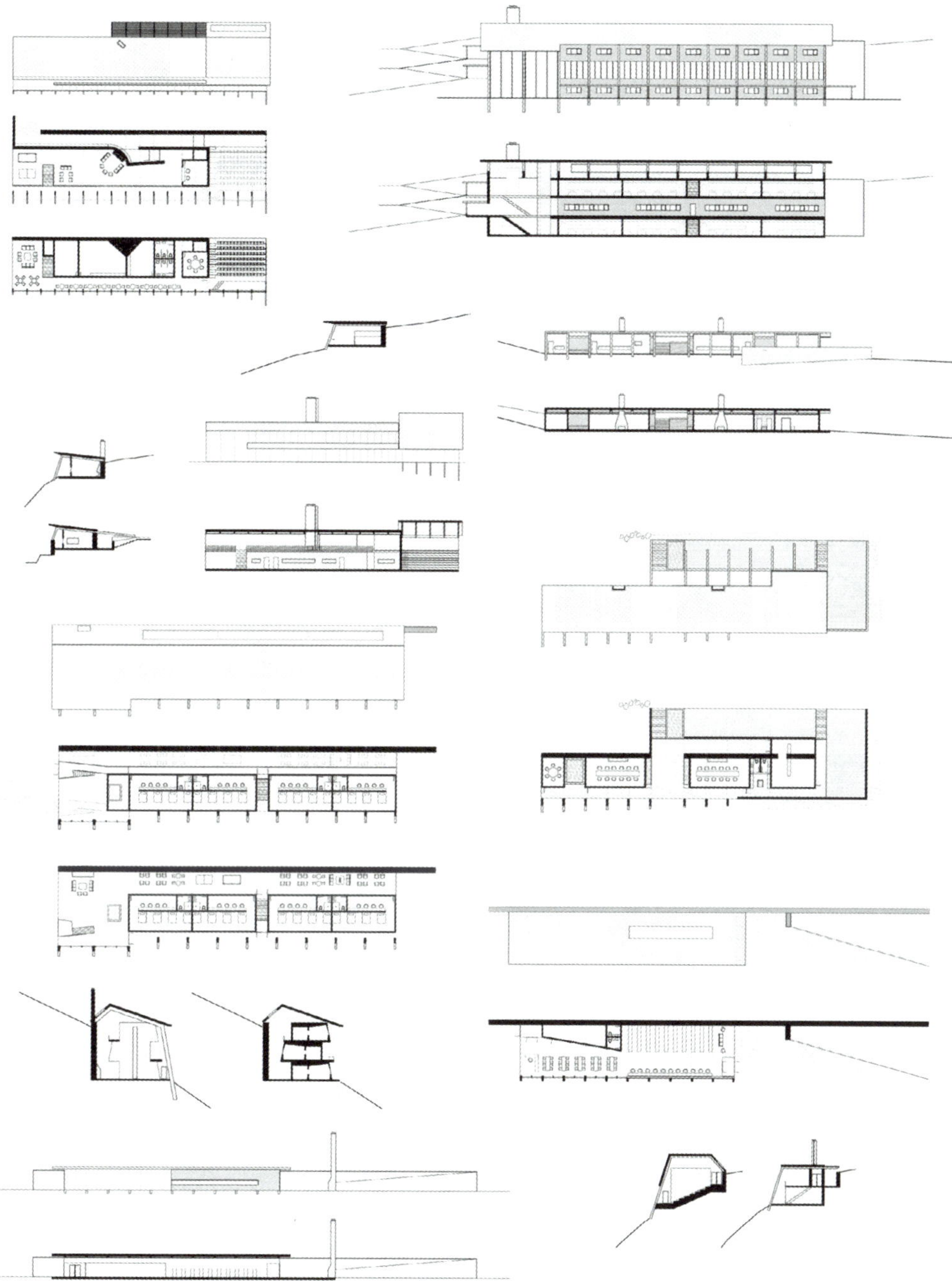

3 Site map as "imaginative geography"

4 Dining lodge referencing vernacular gabled forms

5 Orthographic drawings of seven core lodges

6

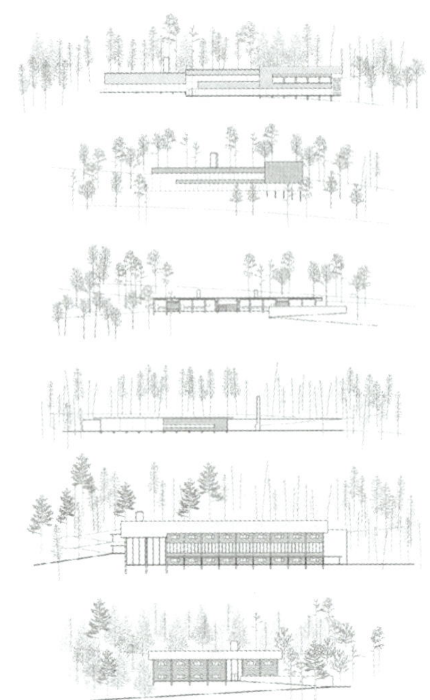

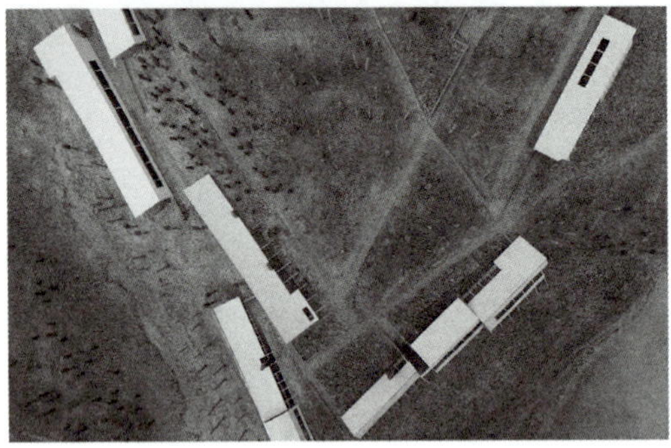

7

6 Buildings lodge into the ground rather than rest upon it.

7 Schematic model

Kate Fisher
Place(s): Camp for Kids

The "summer camp" movement began in the late nineteenth century in the midst of the Progressive Era. Camps started to supplement the home, church, and school as institutions of learning and development, and the term *boyology* was coined to refer to practices established to strengthen the development of young men. It also suggests how summer camps play a role in conditioning and reinforcing certain schemas. By shaping what children do and how they do it, these camps have defined modern childhood. This project challenges normative ideas of summer camp to promote inclusivity and validate difference through architectural forms. It leverages architectural constants to develop a formal language that is recognizable but different. The hearth remains constant across culture and time as a symbol of place. In this project chimney forms suggest habitable space, enclosure, and points of activity on the site.

1

2

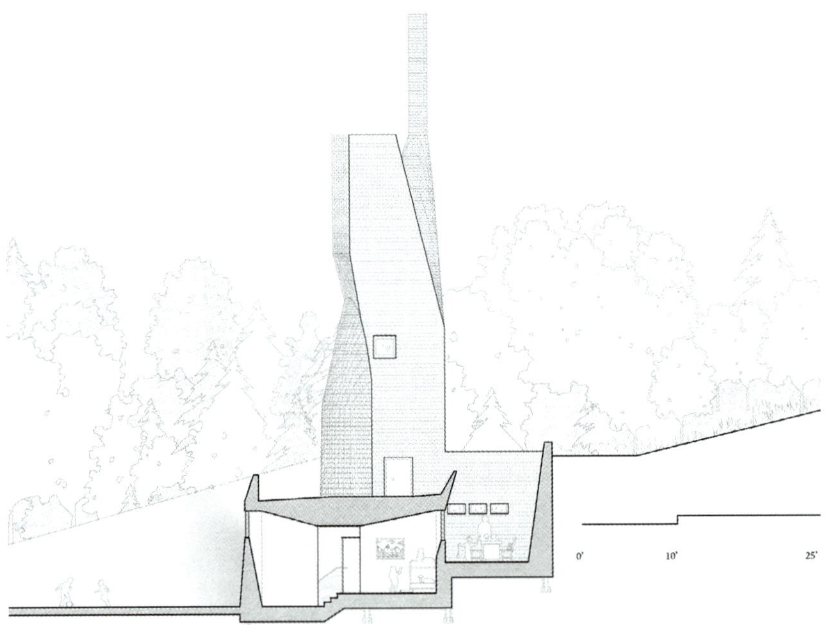

1 Rabbit Snare Gorge Camp, 2018 (previous page)

2 Cross section, pavilion for nine occupants

3 Floor plans, pavilion for nine occupants

4 Final model, pavilion for nine occupants

5 Final model, pavilion for nine occupants

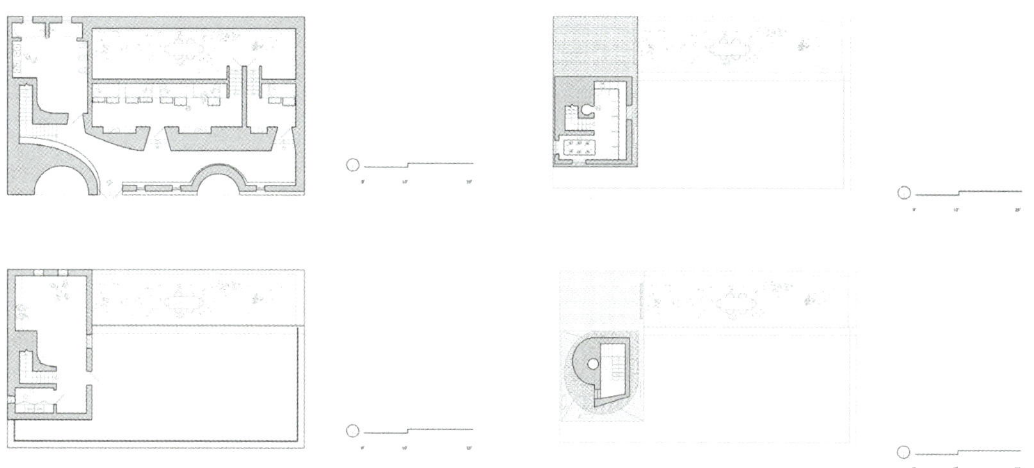

3

4

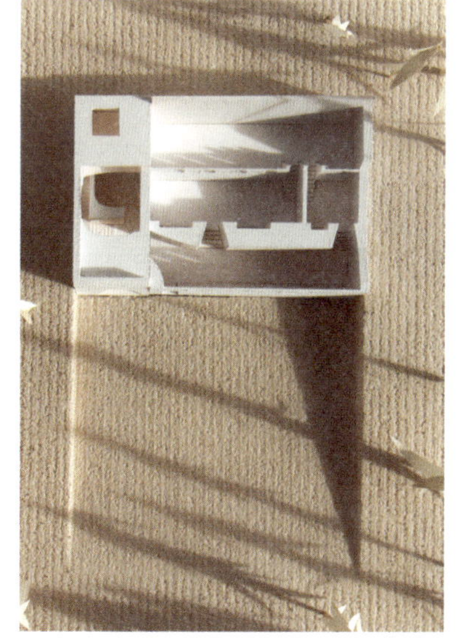

5

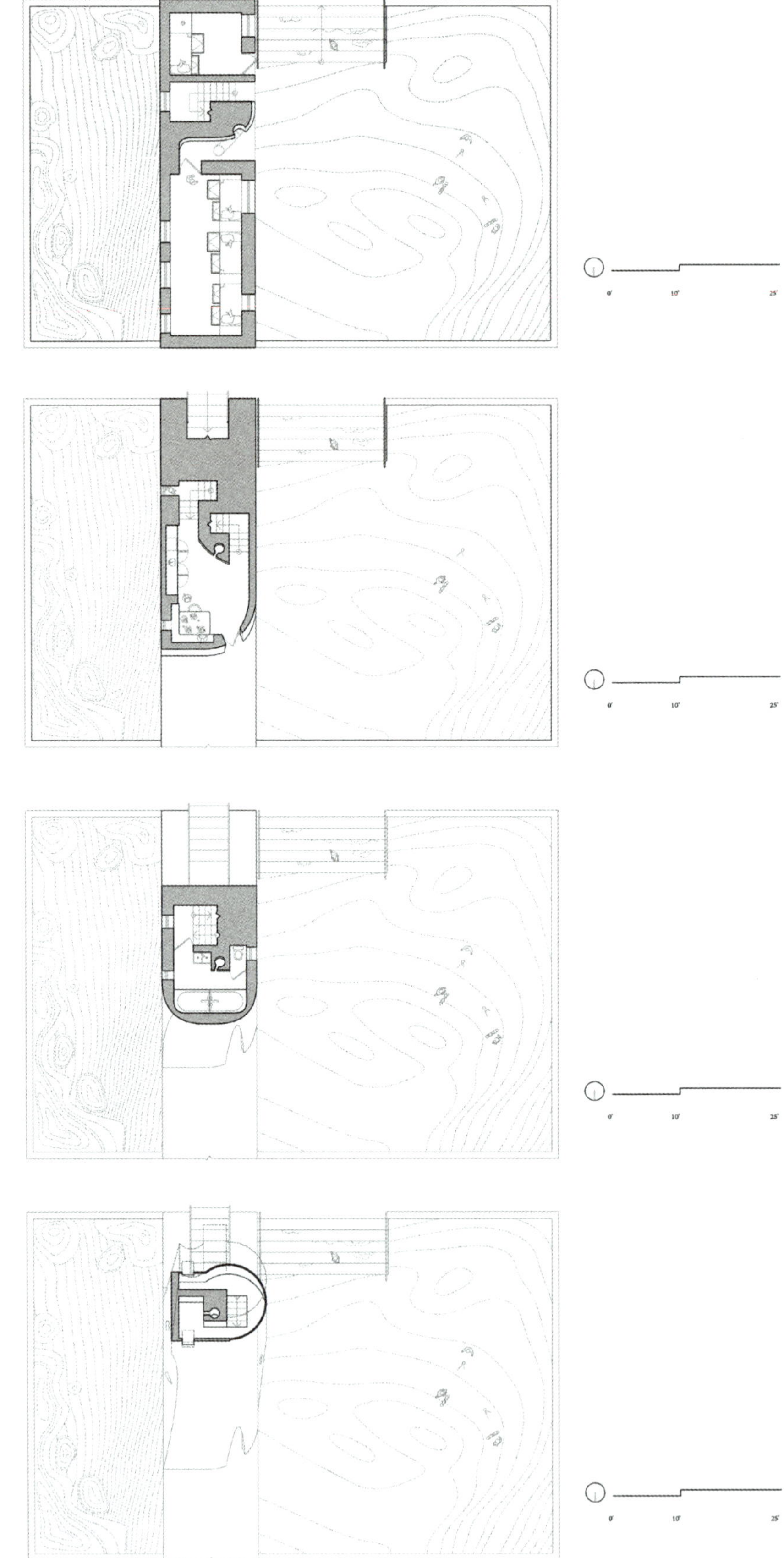
0'
10'
25'
0'
10'
25'
0'
10'
25'
0'
10'
25'

7

8

9

6 Floor plans, pavilion for four occupants

7 Final model, pavilion for nine occupants

8 Process form making

9 Formal chimney study

Colin Sutherland
Interpretative Camp at Rabbit Snare Gorge

The Interpretative Camp at Rabbit Snare Gorge traces the complicated history of human experience and marks its impact on the rugged terrain of Cape Breton Island. Although the dense forests and stunning vistas of Cape Breton are used to advertise it as a place of wild and untamed beauty, in truth this landscape has been greatly modified by the presence of its human occupants. From the relatively light touch of the Mi'kmaq First Nations peoples and the subsistence farms of Acadian and Celtic settlers to the heavy resource extraction of the nineteenth and twentieth centuries, the terrain of Cape Breton carries the scars, both visible and hidden, of its exploitation.

The Interpretative Camp is a place for children to build identities and understand their cultural, material, and environmental heritages. It is organized in a series of four pavilions—the Barn, the Terrace, the Grotto, and the Lookout—arrayed along a cleared path running the length of the site. Each of these hosts an interpretative function and a fraction of the camp's practical infrastructure. Their formation provides both the means of access to the site and a visual axis that reveals the human intervention of construction upon the land. Clearly linking the interior of the site to its waterfront, the path creates a transect through the landscape against which each pavilion must perform an individual architectural response.

1

2

3

4

1 Grotto and path, exterior view

2 Early conceptual drawing: transect as site clearing

3 Barn

4 Terrace, interior view

5

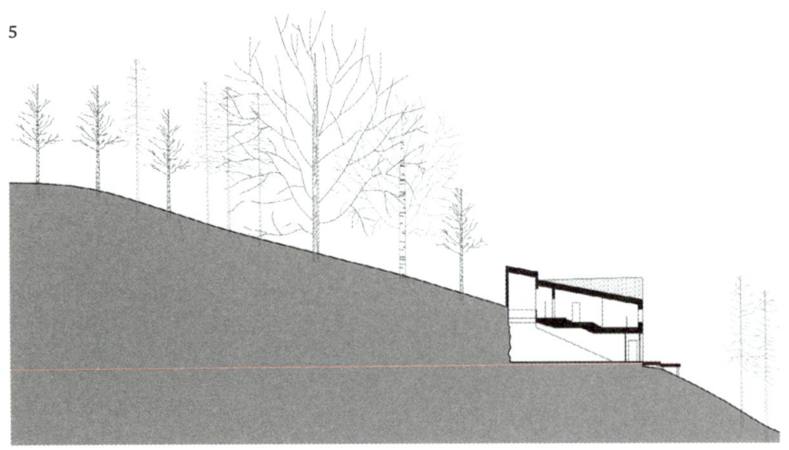

6

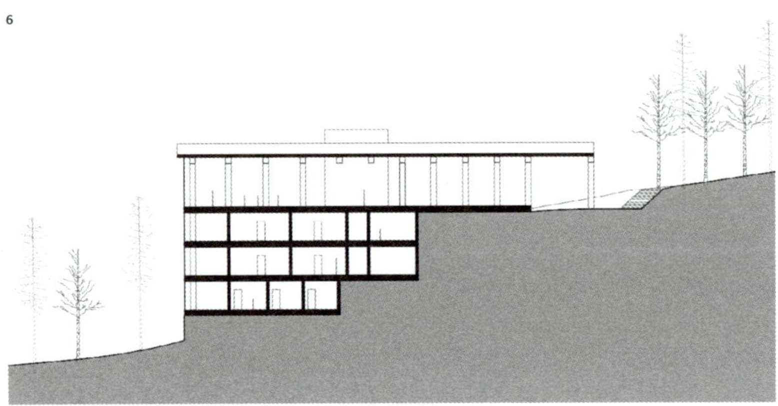

7

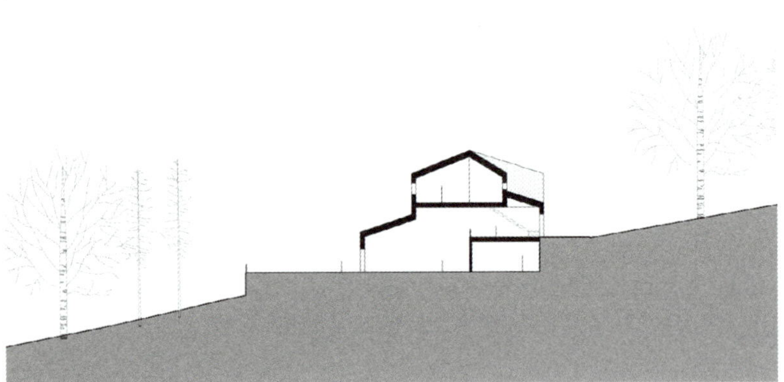

5 Grotto section

6 Terrace section

7 Barn section

8 Site overview

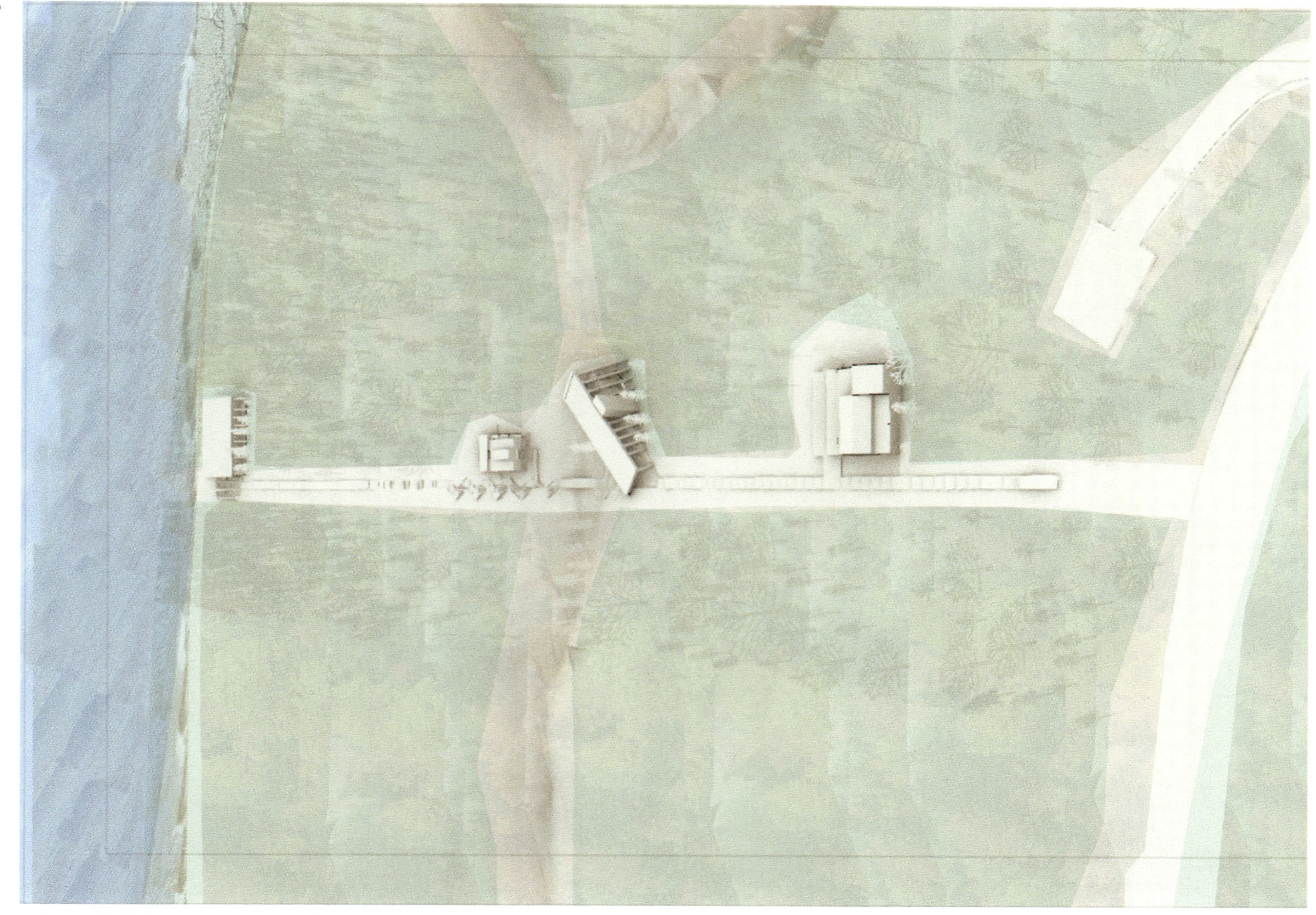

Haylie Chan
Campus of Creatures

The metric of human time is disrupted by the vastness of the landscape, and the various rhythms of the waves, the trees, and the expansive horizon instill in us a different understanding of space. If we think back to our childhood, we may remember wanting to grow up quickly in order to do things only adults were allowed to do. While trying to understand the complexities of the world around us using the few things we knew, we turned to imagination to fill in the rest. What makes childhood so precious to humankind? Why do children want to grow up so quickly, while adults wish they could slow down the progress of time? How do we decelerate the attitude of growing up?

As a response to the aging population in Nova Scotia, this project explores how to bridge the generational gap between children and adults by rethinking the conventional use of architecture. The project, comprising a nursery home and a summer camp, takes on a linear dimension that acts to slow down the metric of time. It embraces the children's misreading of architecture with the act of play at the building level: a bunk-bed tower, an outdoor TV room, and stairs that function as movable seats. The project also encourages "unlearning" for the elderly through spontaneous meetings with young visitors. At the scale of the site, the project acts a mediator between the calmness of the center and the chaos of the forest, serving as the protector of the community.

1

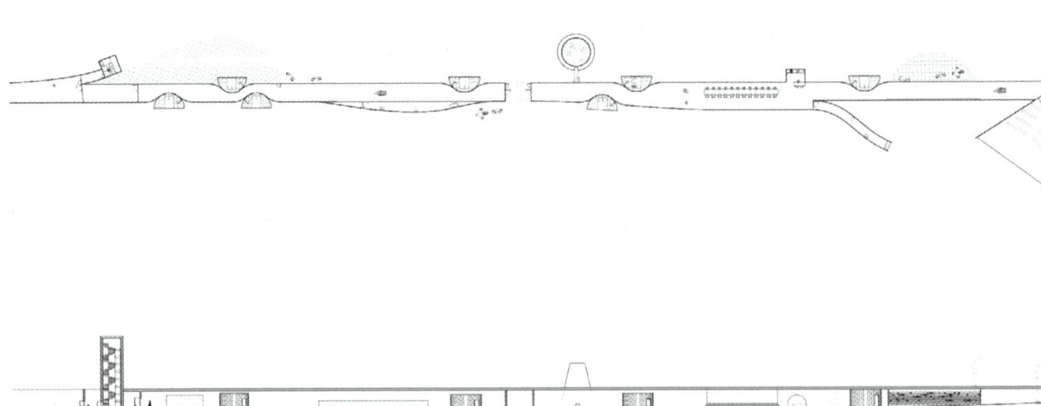

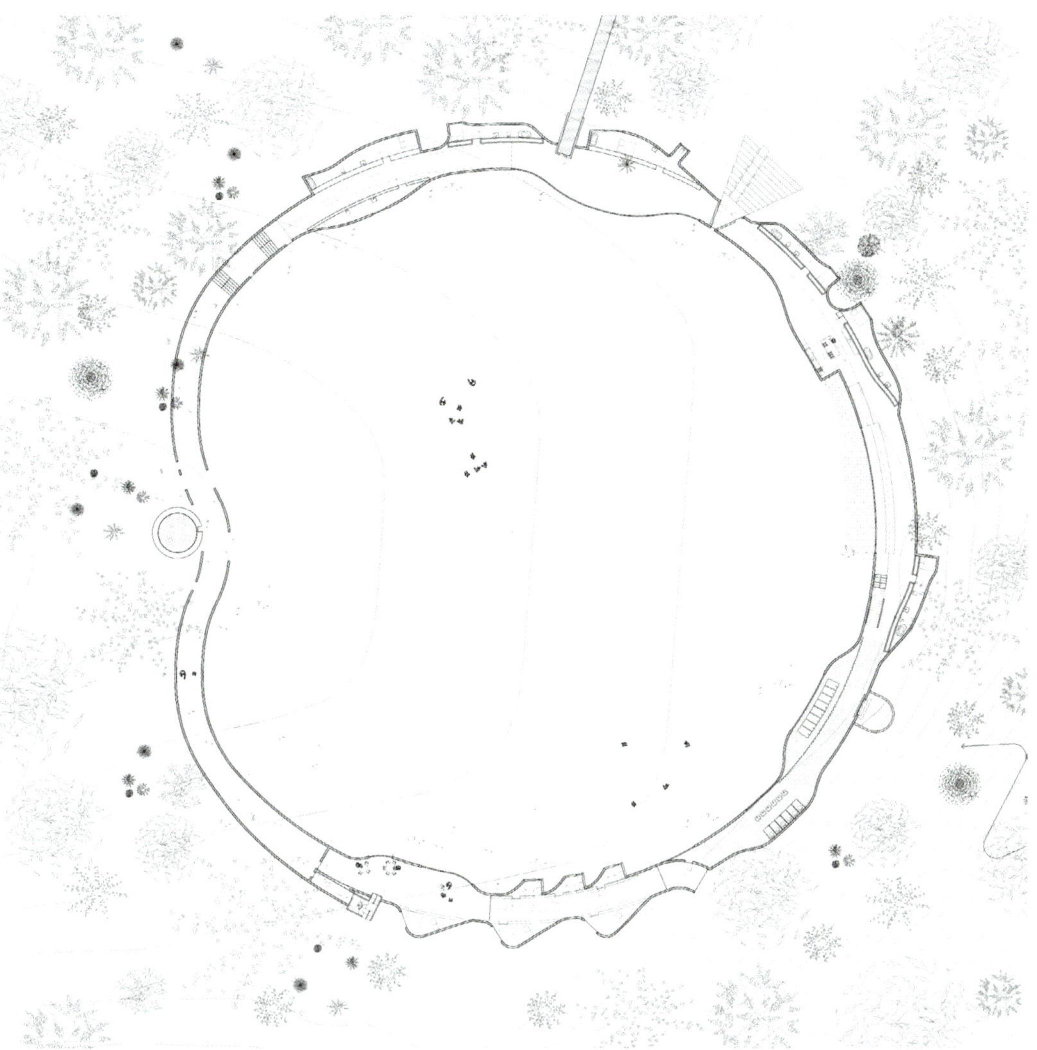

2

1 Unrolled plan and section

2 Plan

3

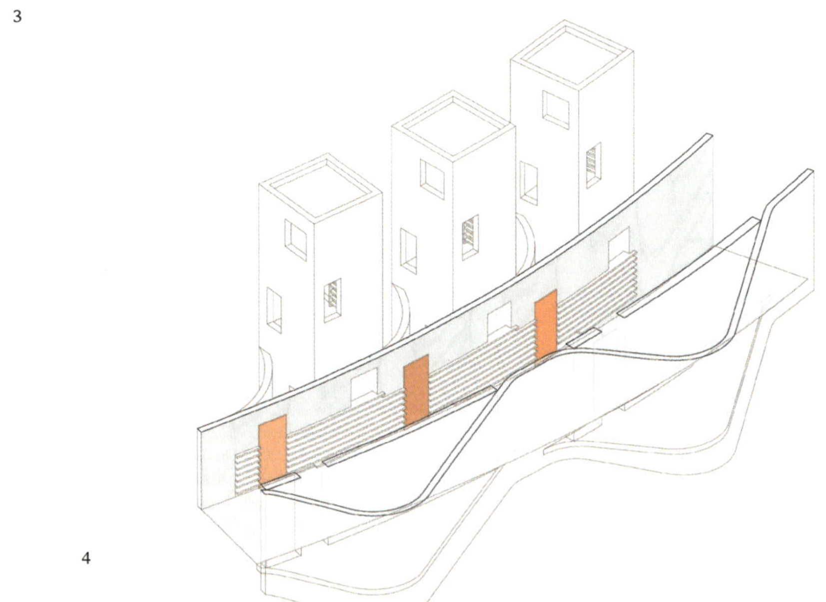

4

5

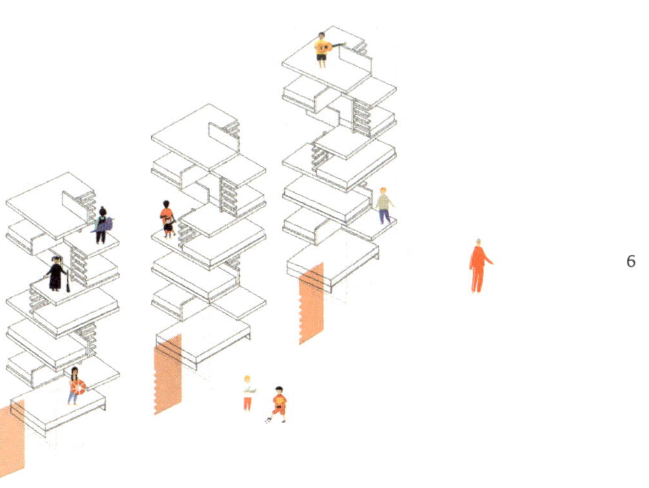

6

3 Interior view, dining room and stair to attic

4 Model

5 Bookshelf

6 Bunk-bed towers

Jincy Kunnatharayil
Campus of Creatures: Habitats in the Wilderness

The project explores the meaning of the word *presence* in the context of architecture. Presence as a tactile ground in proximity and through the concept of "nearness" is a fundamental aspect of the human experience. The project attempts to create a place where kids can physically manifest in the world, connecting with space and time. It is a place designed to form a sense of existence and presence, where the built environment and nature become indecipherable. Taking advantage of natural terrain, built volumes are integrated into the landscape, both hiding and framing it. Spaces are in a constant state of flux, not just mimicking but also becoming nature.

This campus of creatures comprises extended habitats of water, wind, and woods that move without boundaries or borders. Buildings that are intrinsic to the environment provide moments of existential contemplation that make us more self-aware. The days and seasons are expressed in the temporal scales of the walls, a niche, and the large roofs. Wet stones, weathered wood, and moss on the walls create a continuum that resonates at a deeper level and allows us to escape into another temporal space. The expression of weathering on the pavilion surfaces emphasizes nature's presence.

1

2

1 Process sketches

2 Site plan

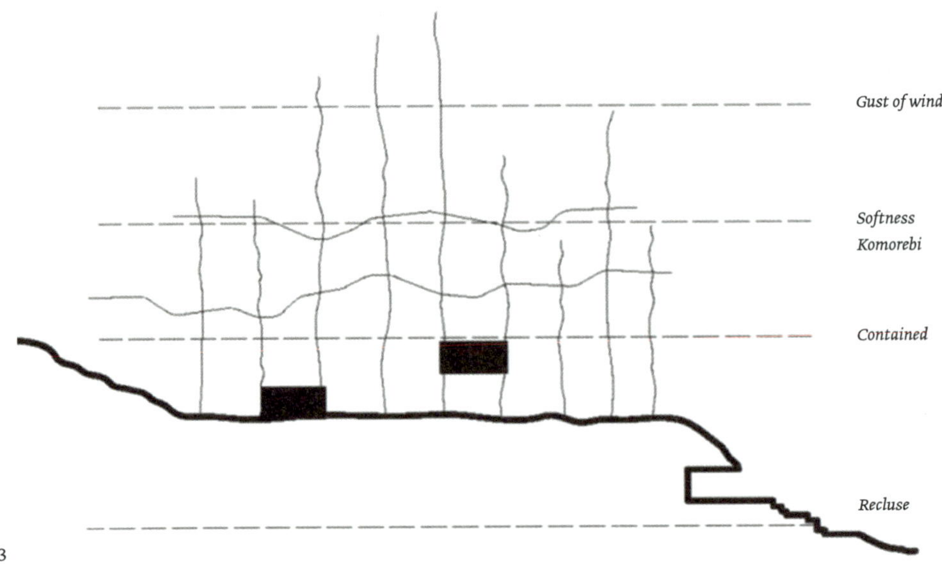

3

4

5

5

6

7

3 Concept diagram

4 Site strategy diagram

5 Sectional view of studio pavilion

6 Section of sleep pavilion

7 Views of sleep pavilion

8 Plan of sleep pavilion

Katherine Barymow
A Path Apart

Traversing the landscape of Rabbit Snare Gorge is a humbling feat. Most of its hills are insurmountable to the unequipped amateur, and in extreme rain and wind even walkable areas of the terrain present a challenge of physical endurance. Yet we struggle forward partially for the sake of hubris but mostly because every few hundred feet we are rewarded with a picturesque view of the ocean in the distance. As we complete the inevitable descent, we meet the water's humbling horizon spanning infinitely toward the edge of the Earth. At Rabbit Snare Gorge Earth Sciences Camp students learn about geology, trees, birds, and whales in the pavilions that dot the landscape. A path runs seamlessly among the pavilions, engaging in the landscape at, below, and above the ground to give students a unique sectional experience of the terrain and ecosystem.

Students receive practical training in the focused programs while garnering a curated set of sensory experiences in the virgin landscape. The experience begins at the crossing of the two creeks, where students can walk freely between the residence hall, auditorium, and dining hall. Here the path takes on elaborate roles in the spatial definition of congregational space as well as a system for rain and wind protection. The path dwindles down to the forms of pavement and a railing, allowing students to traverse the difficult terrain and gain novel spatial readings of the environment through its modulation with respect to the ground plane. The path caps at the cliff's edge, where it transforms into a staircase leading down to the water and facilitating whale observation on an intimate level.

1

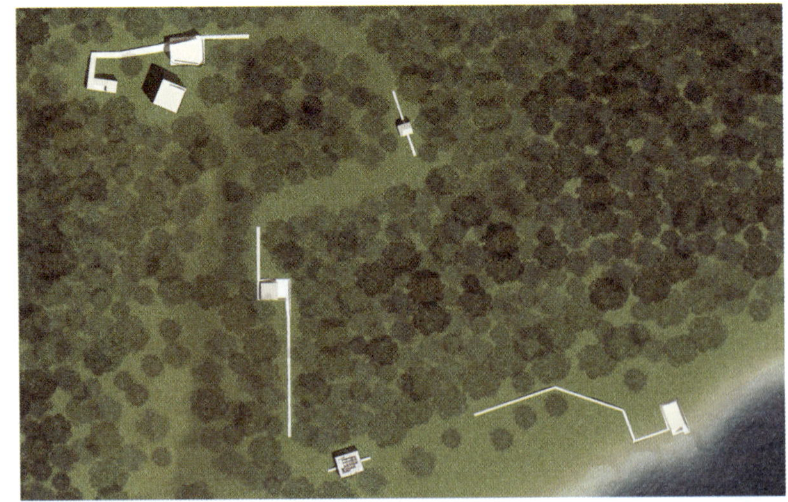

2

3

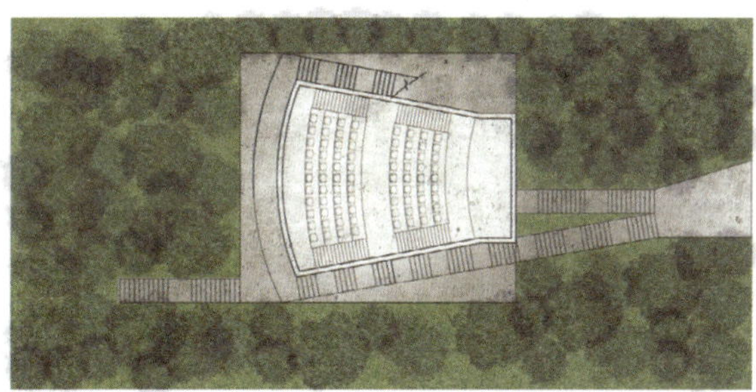

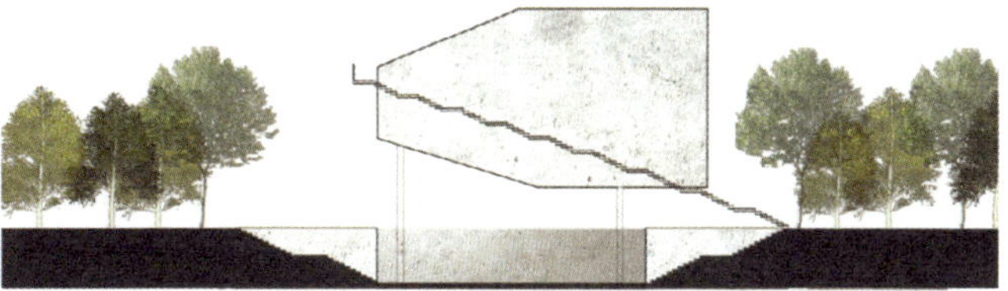

1 Site plan showing pavilions that give visitors a sectional experience of the terrain

2 Bird-watching pavilion

3 Gathering-hall schematics

4

5

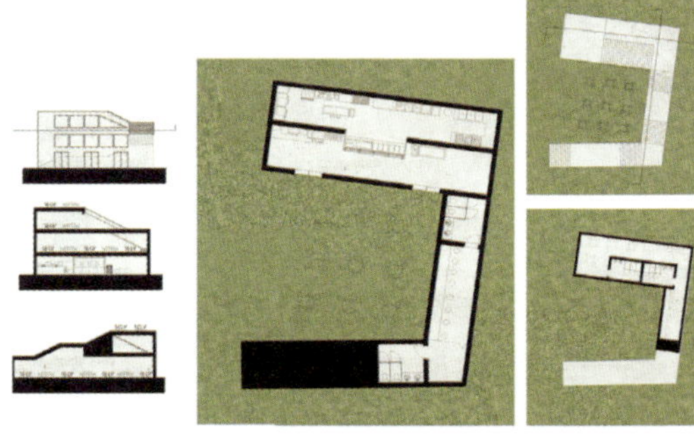

6

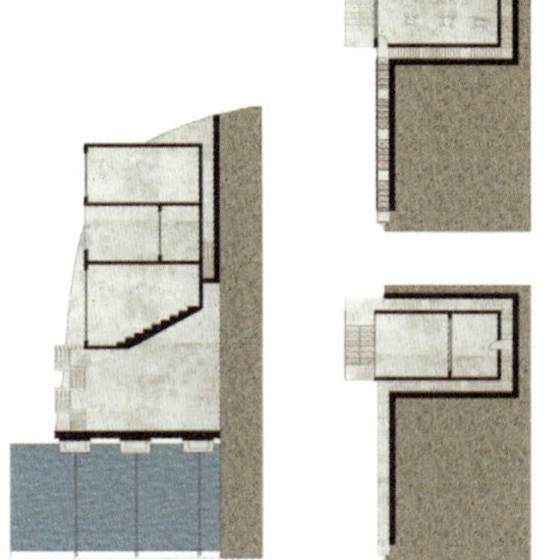

4 Whale-watching pavilion

5 Geology pavilion schematics

6 Whale-watching pavilion schematics

7 Tree-viewing pavilion

8 Geology pavilion

7

8

Lara AlKhouli
Off the Grid

Off the Grid is a year-round technology-free wellness retreat nestled on the remote Cape Breton Island, in Nova Scotia. Located on forty-seven acres of untouched wilderness, it provides campers of ages eight to sixteen the opportunity to reconnect with themselves and their peers while teaching them how to connect with nature.

Inspired by the Lost Boys in *Peter Pan*, the architectural design challenges convention with cabins placed in niches between trees. Spaces are taken from voids left between the foliage and the wood cabins, which push the boundaries of the domestic dwelling in their harmony within the forest. They function both inwardly and outwardly, allowing the forest to enter the interior space. The design allows the children to immerse themselves in nature, introducing them to the different local species. Through daily activities, the camp also teaches personal skills and a sense of independence.

1

2

1 Schematic site model

2 Sleeping cabins imagined as tree houses in densely wooded areas

3 Cabins elevated from the ground plane to create space among the trees

4 Experiential view of the campus

3

4

5

5 Collage, relationship of natural and human site occupation

6

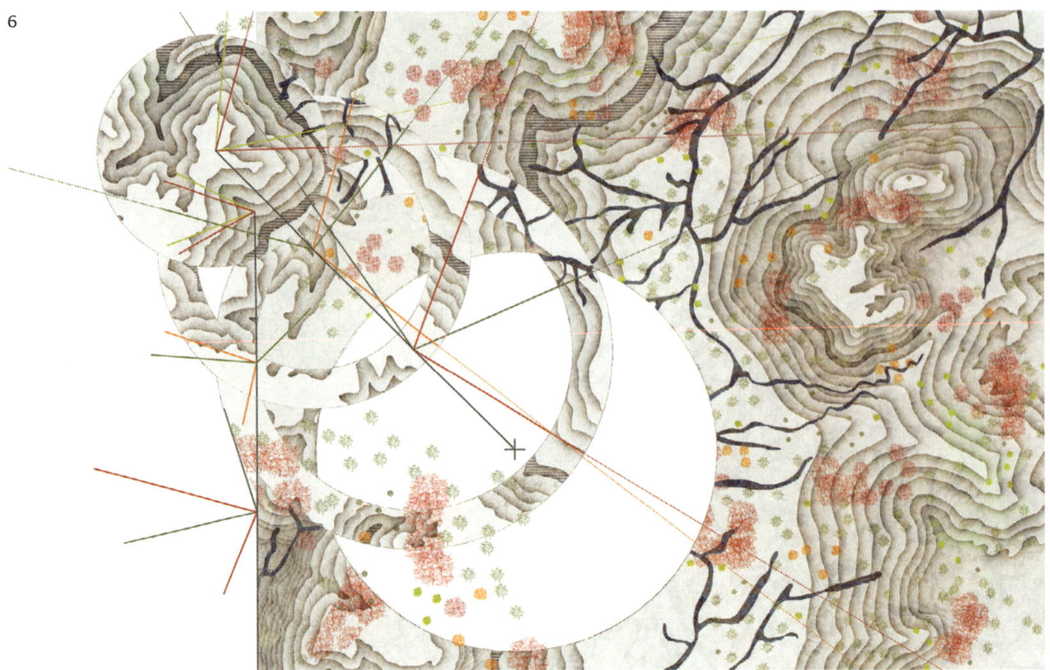

7

8

6 Camp relating to the natural land formations and watersheds

7 Longitudinal section, relation of camp programs to site (part 1)

8 Longitudinal section, relation of camp programs to site (part 2)

9 Index of architectural and spatial elements

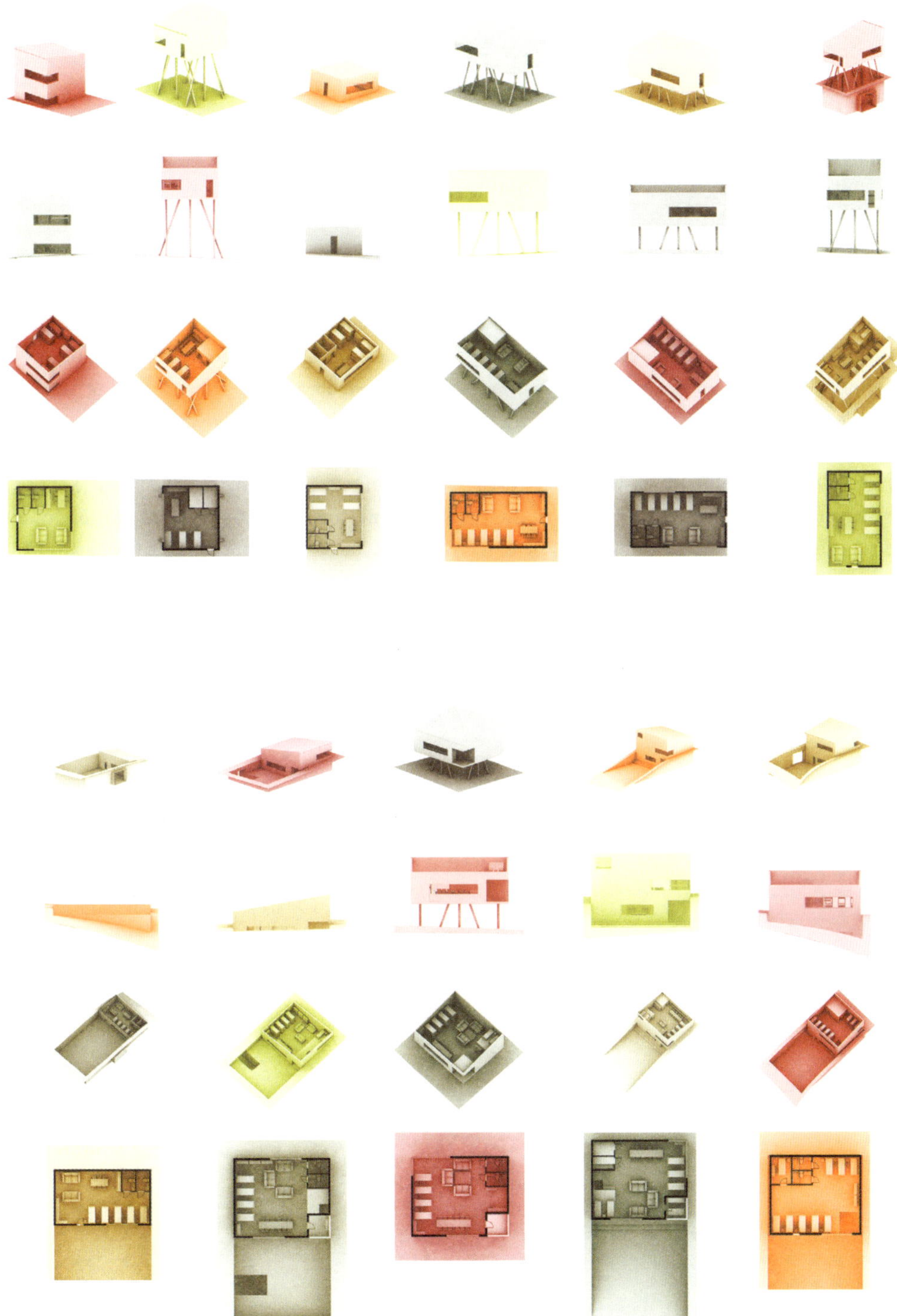

Nino Boornazian
Camp Clearing

The site strategy identifies three zones of interest—plateau, ravine, and coast—corresponding to gathering, adventure, and aquatic activities. The inevitable descent to the coast through the site is syncopated with moments of total immersion in vegetation. Moments of compression and release are synchronized to enhance the potency of their distilled effects. An expansive view of the ocean is appreciated more when discovered after emerging from a thick brush. This craft-centric camp provides occupational and educational opportunities to local residents and visiting campers. The crafts instructions respond to Cape Breton's cultural identity and harness the skills of local residents. The buildings take advantage of the dynamic topography and varied site conditions to provide spaces that celebrate the beauty of their surroundings.

1 Sited experiential diagram indicating moments of syncopation

2 Site plan

1

Sited Experiential Diagram
50'
100'
1/32" = 1' Scale
2
A
B
13.
10.
9.
11.
8.
5.
6.
7.
1.
2.
3.
4.
Site Plan
1. Housing 7-13
2. Housing 13+
3. Ropes Course
4. Graphics Pavilion
5. Performing Arts Pavilion
6. Ceramics Pavilion
7. Carpentry Pavilion
8. Administration
9. Cafeteria
10. Gallery
11. Meadow
13 Parking
50'
100'
1/32" = 1' Scale

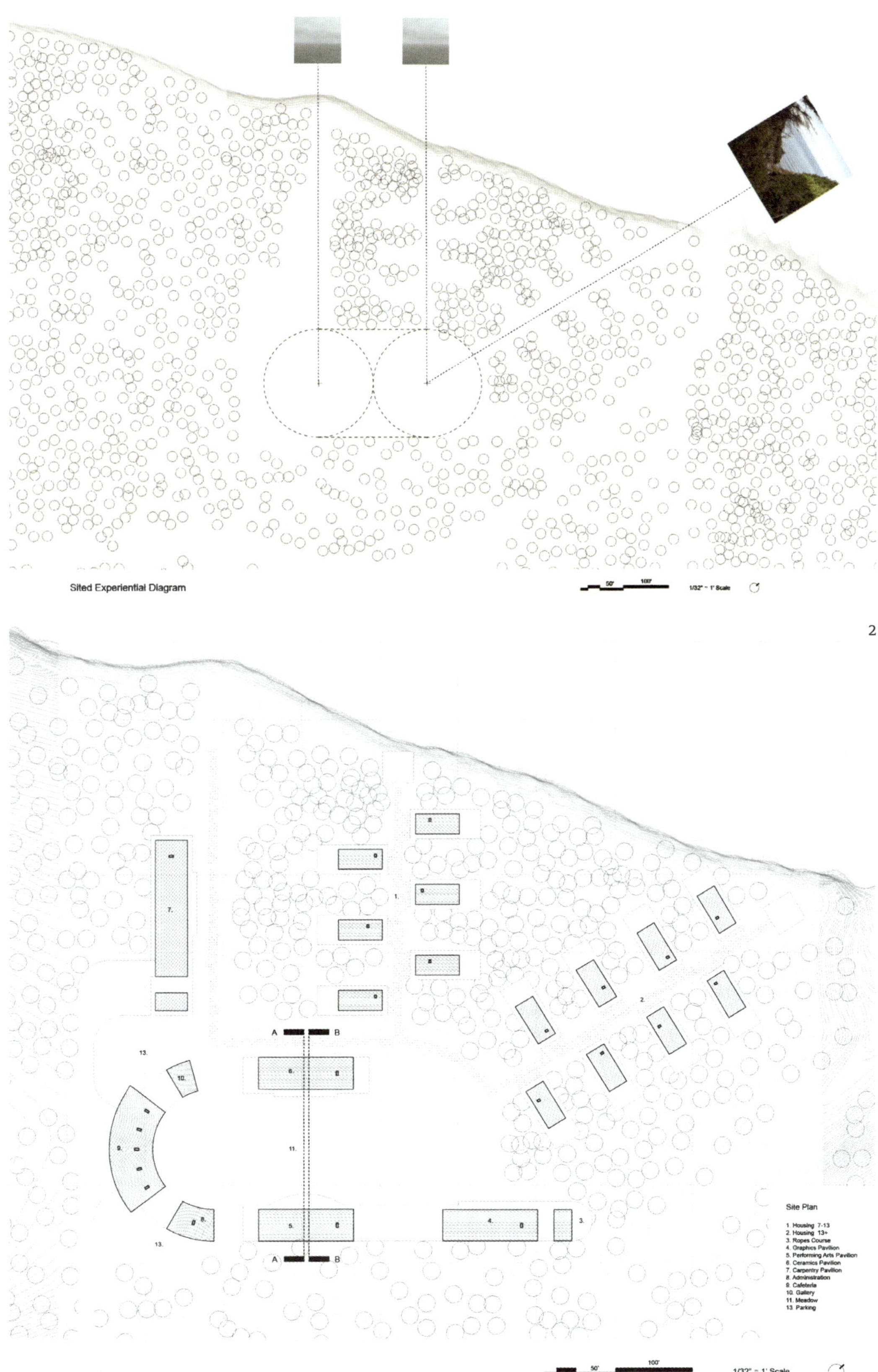

3

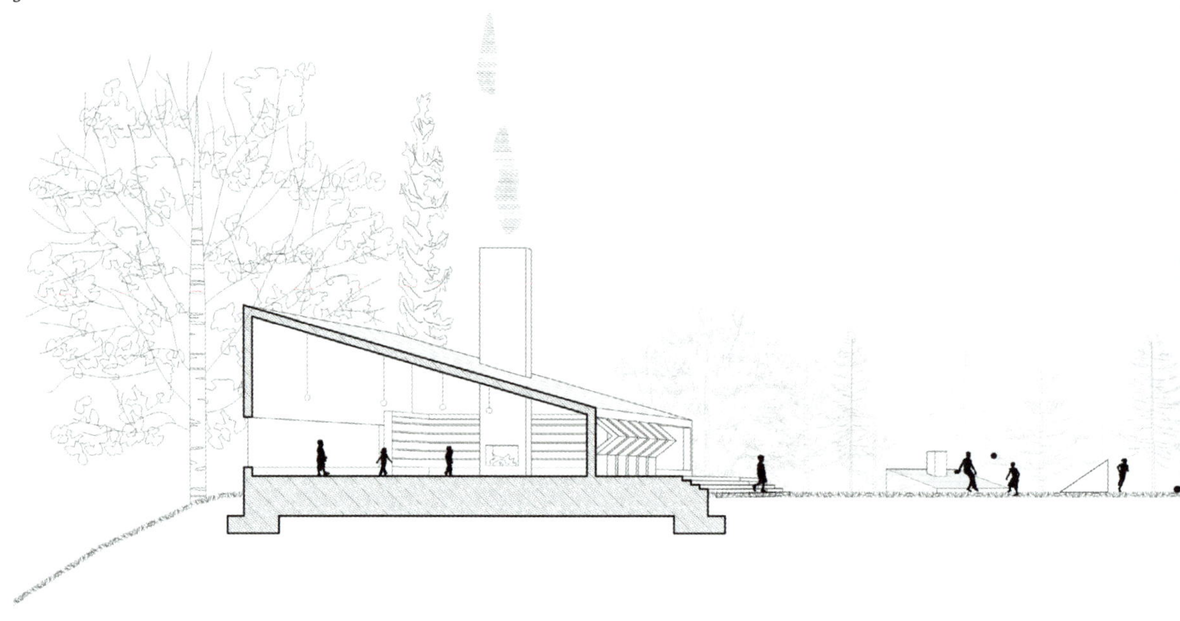

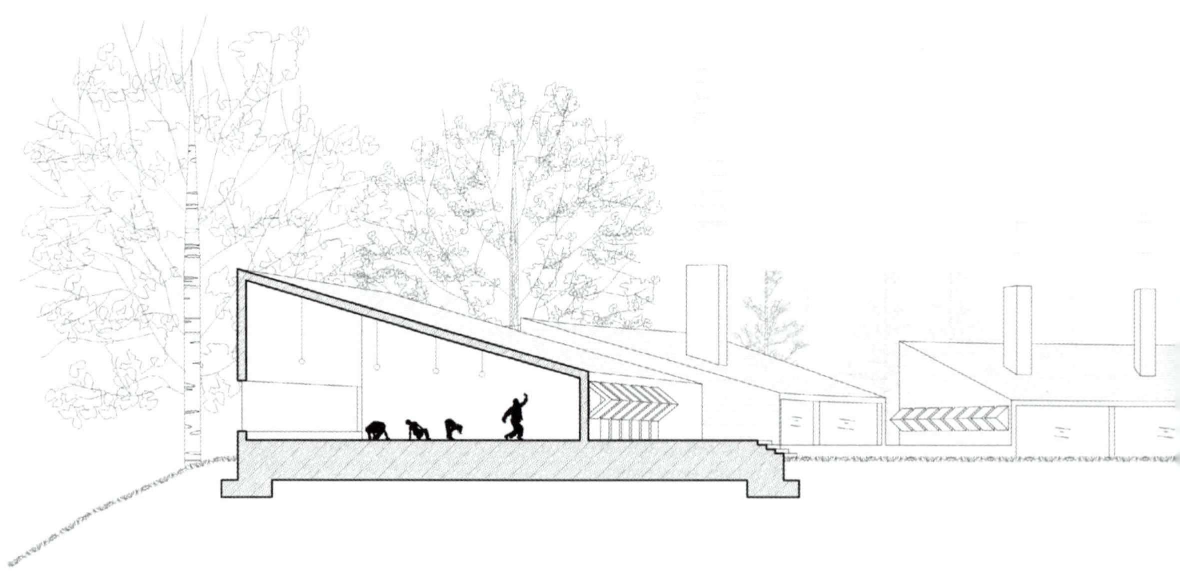

3 Mirrored section perspective cut through center of meadow

Ryan Hughes
The Forum

Artists have long sought creative strength through immersion in nature. The Forum generates collective gathering in a monumental landscape. Proposed as a creative arts camp for children, the project is sited on fifty acres of oceanfront in Inverness, Nova Scotia. Arrived at through a series of topographic investigations, the architecture attempts to establish a new ground plane. Sited with a delicate relationship to the topography, the living pavilion sits atop the crest of the site.

A logarithmic pattern of indoor and outdoor space is projected from a new horizontal datum four feet above grade at its minimum and thirty-two feet above at its maximum. The play between the ground and the projected pattern generates a dynamic system of space that changes in plan and section simultaneously. Campers use the volume as a place for the exchange of ideas, formation of new relationships, and reconsideration of the landscape.

1

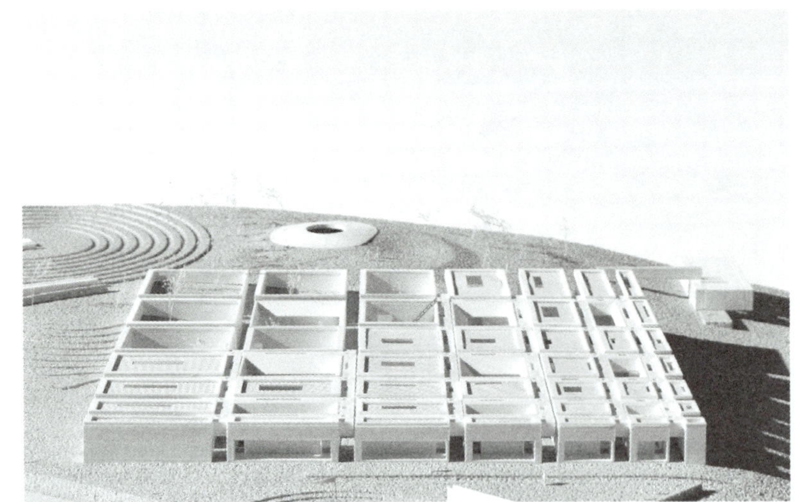

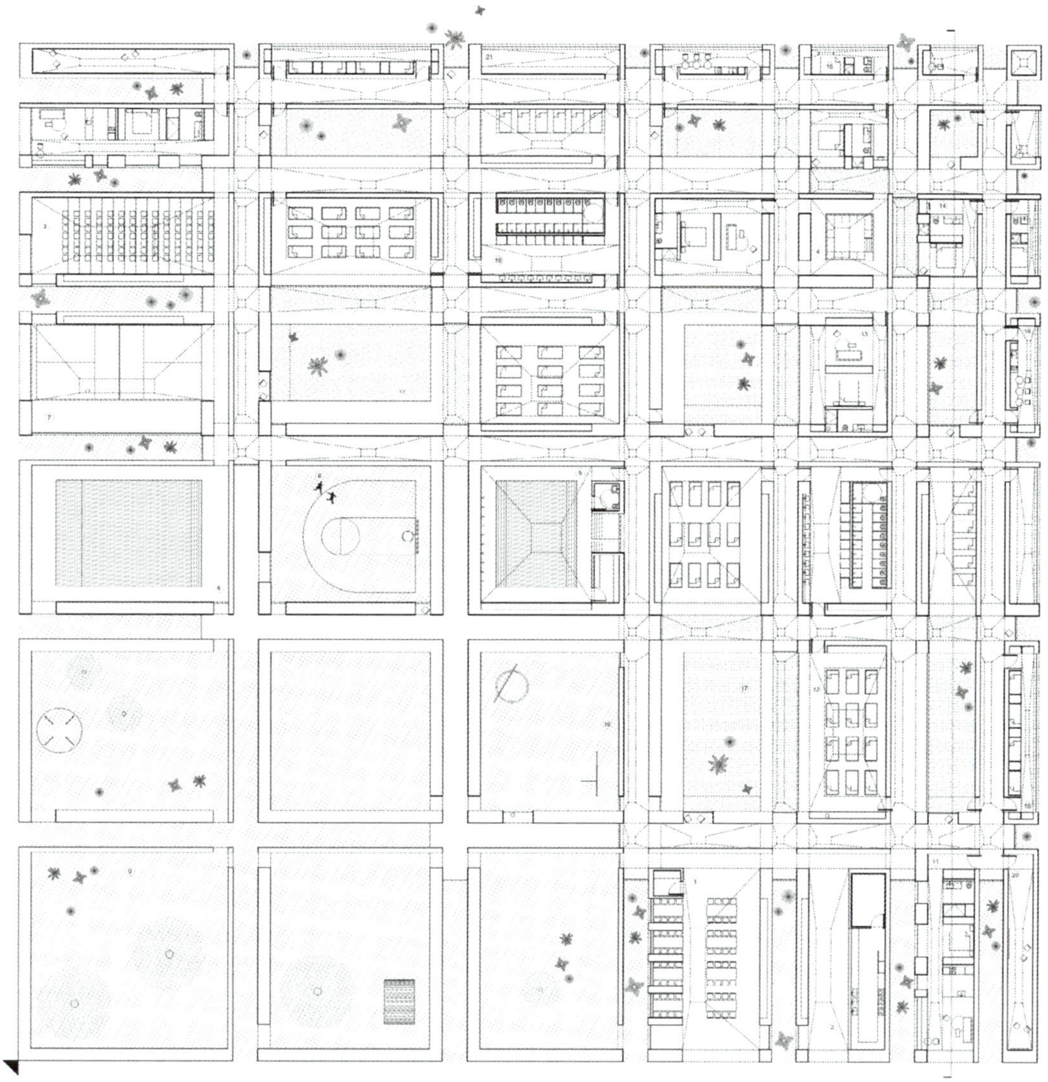

2

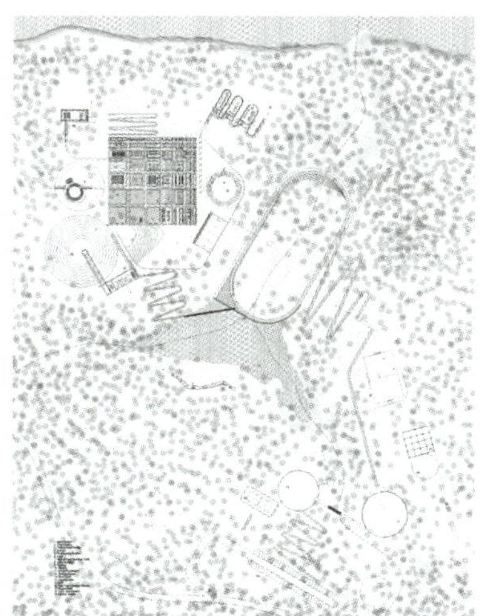

3

1 Model

2 Plan of main pavilion for living and working

3 Site plan showing topographical manipulations

4

5

6

4 View toward the living pavilion

5 Corner of living pavilion

6 South elevation of living pavilion

7

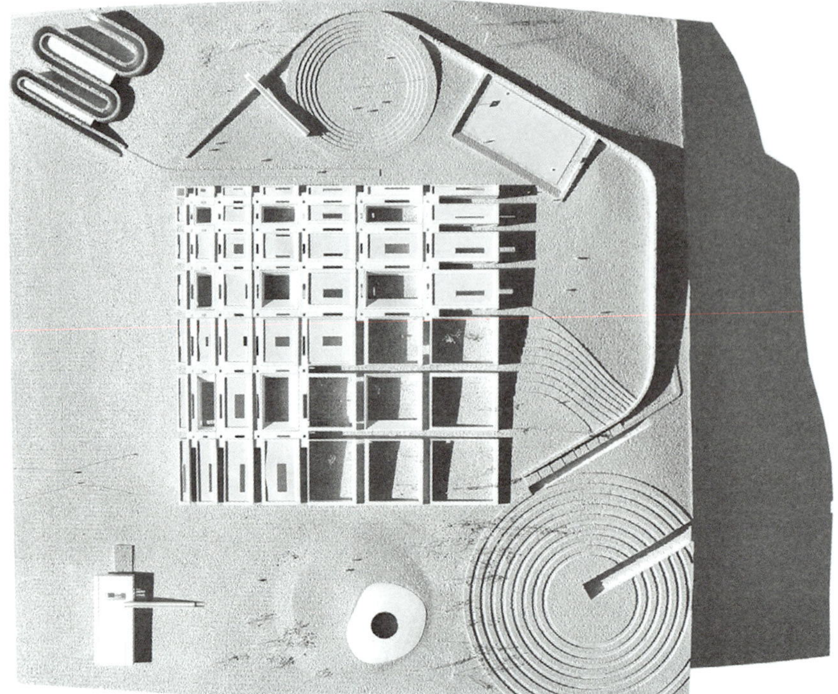

8

7 Schematic model detail

8 Schematic model detail

Sunny Cui
Down the Rabbit Hole

I followed the rabbit down this hole.

The Maze
One step down the rabbit hole,
There is no sky, nor ground.
Darkness, it has been found, is composed
Of infinite number of rooms
Along the monotonous and the fluid.
To whom it borders, to whom it unites.
To the hunters who stop by, to the fishermen
who said hi.
Now you see the opening to the far behind,
"Leave the capsule if you dare.
Your quest starts from here."

The Roof (a Hearth)
The kitchen tour takes longer than expected,
Fitted out the tables run in a spiral, a small square.
Here we wait in lines,
I am kept warm in the hearth
Though I am almost starving to death.
The roof floats over the room.
The view turns the outside into a slowly moving still.

The Tower
Waistline down the rabbit hole,
What better manifesto to this dream than a thin
and infinite line,
A bridge between the Earth and the Sun.
Each level is a wink that closes and opens
up the eyes,
Views that change every step,
Hidden in the smallest of details and the tiniest
thresholds,
There is a new world behind every sign.

The Wall
The great plateau lies behind,
The mountain in front too dangerous to climb,
A grand door narrowed it down to a single thought.
I must climb up the stairs,
Till I reach the top,
Of this endless trail.
Swings, bars, ropes, and pipes,
Anything that dropped from my pocket,
Makes the profoundest chord.
I can't see the top,
I can't find the bottom,
Which way is up?
Which way is down?
Growing strong.

This poem that I wrote, and a navigation map will be given to visiting kids as tools for role-playing. The buildings on the site are counterparts of the landscape and "nonplayer characters" that breathe and communicate to the kids. The project starts with the Cubes, a basic architectural element of the fundamental form of dwelling. But these artificial forms stand, move, and collapse. In this game they shape oppression and compression; and create comfort and anxiety: a sunken floor for sleeping, a self-supported roof for dining, an endlessly rising column for activities, a thickened wall for training, and a nonenclosure for contemplating. On the site map there are many abstract cubes that work as platforms or fragmented pieces in which to live immersed in nature. The project recreates a narrative from anecdotes that we experienced or heard on our studio visit to Nova Scotia, and these spaces recall the activities that kids at camp will conquer through quests and obstacles, finally finding their way to dwell in nature.

1

2

3

4

5

1 Site plan

2 Maze, section, and plan

3 Wall, section, and plan

4 Tower, section, and plan

5 Roof, section, and plan

6

7

8

9

6 Maze, interior

7 Maze, final model

8 Tower, elevation, seen from the brook

9 Wall, final model, with open roof

10

10 Tower, final model

Image Credits

Omar Gandhi Architect: 4, 5, 6, 7, 9, 15, 16, 17

Benjamin Olsen: 22, 23, 24 (top), 26, 27, 28, 29, 30

Kate Fisher: 31, 32, 33, 34, 35

Colin Sutherland: 24 (bottom), 36, 37, 38, 39

Haylie Chan: 40, 41, 42, 43

Jincy Kunnatharayil: 44, 45, 46, 47

Katherine Barymow: 48, 49, 50, 51

Lara AlKhouli: 52, 53, 54-55, 56, 57

Nino Boornazian: 59, 60-61

Ryan Hughes: 62, 63, 64, 65, 66

Sunny Cui: 68, 69, 70, 71, 72

SCOTT RUFF

Gullah Geechee Institute